DATE DUE

79		

CHAUCER
AT OXFORD AND AT
CAMBRIDGE

CHAUCER
AT OXFORD AND AT CAMBRIDGE

J. A. W. BENNETT

UNIVERSITY OF TORONTO PRESS

First published 1974 in Canada and the
United States by University of Toronto Press
Toronto and Buffalo

ISBN 0 8020 2155 7
LC 74 81706

This book has been published with the help of a
grant from the Humanities Research Council
of Canada using funds provided by the
Canada Council

Printed in Great Britain
at the University Press, Oxford
by Vivian Ridler
Printer to the University

PREFACE

THESE studies represent the Alexander Lectures that I had the honour of delivering before the University of Toronto in December 1970. In print they may seem an inadequate return for Canadian kindness. But possibly some compensation for the deficiencies of their oral form will be found in the Notes and Appendices that publication enables me to provide.

J. A. W. B.

CONTENTS

ABBREVIATIONS

BPR   *Register of the Black Prince* (HMSO 1930–3)

BRUO *Biographical Register of the University of Oxford to A.D. 1500* (A. B. Emden, Oxford, 1957–9)

CAS   *Proceedings of the Cambridge Antiquarian Society*

CT   *The Canterbury Tales*

EETS Publications of the Early English Text Society

OHS   Publications of the Oxford Historical Society

I

LIFE AND LEARNING IN ROLLS AND RECORDS

I BEGIN by removing a possible misapprehension. By 'Chaucer at Oxford and at Cambridge' I mean, simply: Chaucer at Oxford and at Cambridge, and I shall chiefly be considering the roles that his clerks play in either place. With Chaucerian studies at these universities I have no concern. Not that they would prove an unrewarding topic: for if Chaucer did not begin at Oxford, Chaucerian scholarship did, in the person of Thomas Tyrwhitt, of Merton and Queen's, first true editor of the *Canterbury Tales*. The only scholar to have surpassed him is Walter W. Skeat, of Christ's College, Cambridge. Tyrwhitt's edition began to appear in 1775, Skeat's 120 years later; and the interval is likely to be as long before there comes such another.

Tyrwhitt lived in Oxford for over ten years, Skeat in Cambridge for over fifty; which makes it the more surprising that neither scholar paid particular attention to the tales set in these towns. Skeat, indeed, thought that Chaucer knew little of Cambridge; but he can hardly have given the matter the three hours that he made a rule of allotting to any such major problem. His affable ghost, or Tyrwhitt's, might well assert that in his time, when it came to university or collegiate history, it was still difficult to separate fact from fiction. But the great 'three-deckers' associated with the names of Willis and Clark in the one place and Rashdall in the other have changed all that; and the patient work of Stokes and Salter, Gunther and Pantin,

Powicke and M. R. James has yielded a harvest of exemplary monographs, well-edited documents, detailed catalogues, and architectural reports. Dr. Emden's great biographical registers, covering both universities up to 1500, have set new standards of fullness and accuracy, besides providing bases for inquiries into the local origins and later careers of medieval students. Wholesale demolitions, prewar and postwar, have actually added to our knowledge of medieval Oxford. The surveys of both towns sponsored by the Institute for Historical Research and the Historical Monuments Commission have now been published. Dr. Graham Pollard has lectured on the earliest Oxford statutes and Fr. M. B. Hackett has produced a study of their new-found Cambridge counterpart; whilst only this year (1970) Oxford has embarked on a comprehensive collaborative history. Recently, too, Dr. Cobban has published the results of his detailed investigations into the accounts of a Cambridge hall—probably the one that Chaucer's Reeve had in mind; and his volume follows hard upon Dr. Highfield's edition of the earliest Merton Rolls. I wish that historians could pause more often from transcribing rolls, receipts, and charters, and enlighten us about Cambridge manciples or Oxford parish clerks. But they have excuse for dismissing our literary studies as lightweight if we ignore the documents that they have already put into our hands.

In Chaucerian studies today whoso would do any good —to apply an apophthegm of Blake's—must do it in minute particulars. Yet it is not essential (and it is almost impracticable) to imitate Edith Rickert's feats of endurance at the Public Record Office. For no cities have been better served by their antiquaries than Oxford and Cambridge. Brian Twyne and Anthony Wood in seventeenth-century Oxford, Baker, Bowtell, and Cooper somewhat later in Cambridge, assembled and copied masses of documents (some now lost), and the Oxford Historical Society and the Cambridge Antiquarian Society have put many into print. True, the crabbed Latin of a bursar's roll, the entries in a Grace Book, may not seem easy or rewarding reading. But they conceal particularities of medieval life that never get into coffee-table books on the splendour of the Middle Ages.

Dr. Pantin has said that Mistress Quickly speaks the language of inventories—'Thou didst swear to me upon a parcel-gilt goblet, sitting in my Dolphin chamber, at the round table by a seacoal fire . . .' By the same token, records of the building and maintenance of colleges alert us to homely and domestic detail we might otherwise overlook, though Chaucer did not. We see him savouring such detail when Nicholas, the student of the Miller's Tale, persuades his Oxford landlord to procure 'a knedyng trogh, and after that a tubbe and a kymelyn' (*CT* A 3620–1), and 'good ale in a jubbe' (3628). Outside Chaucer the term 'jub' is found at this date only in the accounts for the 1392 expedition of the poet's patron the Earl of Derby (the future Henry IV): 'et pro uno pare jobbes de iiij galonibus . . .'[1] So the term indicates that the carpenter and his companions would have plenty to drink when the flood came. This is wholly in character: for when Nicholas had asked him for a drink earlier, he 'broghte of myghty ale a *large* quart' (3497); and it bespeaks the Miller's own notorious potations, which his rival the Reeve is to glance at when he makes a Trumpington miller 'drynken evere strong ale atte beste' (4147), and imbibe so deeply that 'as an hors he snorteth in his sleep' (4163). As to that 'kymelyn', it is a term hardly found elsewhere in literature, but the few early occurrences in accounts enlighten us. A roll of Edward I lists a payment 'Stephano le joignur, pro j kembelina subtus cisternam Regis, vijd';[2] so a kimlin could be shallow enough to slide

---

[1] *Expeditions made by Henry Earl of Derby* (Camden Society, 1894), p. 154.
[2] Cit. *Promptorium Parvulorum* (Camden Society, 1843–65), i. 274 n.

under a chest, and was made by a joiner, not a carpenter
—division of labour was well advanced by the fourteenth
century. John would have to buy or borrow one. The next
example known to me (but not to the *Middle English
Dictionary*) is in the accounts of a Merton bursar, and in
a cryptic context that is worth perusal for other reasons:[1]

Item: for wine when letters were put [*reposita*] on [?] the
chest . . . . 3½*d.*
Item, to a *scriptor* [? engraver; but this sense is not recorded
before 1461] who inscribed the letters on the [common]
chest . . . . 3½*d.*
. . . .
Item, for making locks and windows for the Treasury [the
stone-roofed building that still stands in 'Mob' Quad] . 4*d.*
Item, to men making tubs and vats . . . . 12*d.*
Item, for mats to cover the vats . . . . . 7*d.*
Item, to the illuminators of the letters in azure and vermilion 16*d.*

[this evidently refers to the rubrication in the College's *Liber Rubeus,*
the first terrier, or summary of its charters. It is an earlier example
of vermilion than any in the *Oxford English Dictionary*; and the cost
is explained by a Chaucerian couplet in Lydgate:
We may alday oure colour grynde and bete,
Tempre our azour and vermylioun   (*Troy Book* ii. 4717–18)
—which in turn explains Chaucer's own couplet about the decorator
of Diana's temple in the Knight's Tale:

Wel koude he peynten lifly that it wroghte;
With many a floryn he the hewes boghte.   (A 2087–8)]

Then comes the last and pertinent entry:

Item, for a tub [*cuva*] and for repair of kimlins [*correctura
kimilinorum*] . . . . 12*d.*

These kimlins must be trays or troughs used in the
college hall or kitchen. The term is found in an inventory
of goods found in the college of Goddys hous (Christ's
College, Cambridge) in 1451, after the death of William

---

[1] OHS N.S. xviii. 221 ('before 17 Oct. 1288–Feb. 1289').

Byngham, 'lately Proctor of the same'.[1] Other records indicate that kimlins were also used in brew-houses; Oxford had a whole street of brewers.

I take at random another term, this time from the Cambridge tale. The miller in that story carries 'a Sheffeld thwitel' in his hose (3933). Editors dutifully comment on the reputation of Sheffield steel. The word 'thwitel' is poorly evidenced, and three scribes make nonsense of it; but examples I have come across in fourteenth-century records are revealing: they all concern brawls (one actually at Trumpington) in which a man is killed by his opponent's 'thwitel'.[2] We should evidently think of the miller's hose as his holster. This 'market-betere' was quick on the draw.

One last example, of a different kind. The Cambridge tale is an extended commentary on a line that characterizes the Miller of the Prologue: 'Wel koude he stelen corn, and tollen thries' (A 562). It was a traditional charge against millers that they took more than their duc of the grain they ground, by way of payment, and we usually let it go at that. But the double edge of the line is considerably sharpened when in the Oxford Book of Freemen (Hanasters) we find a claim being brought against the town millers by one John Lewis 'as well for the takinge and distreyninge of three quarters of wheat meale under the pretence and color of a thing forfayte as for the untrewe and excessyve tollinge of certayne quarters of wheat

---

[1] A. H. Lloyd, *The Early History of Christ's College Cambridge* (1934), p. 127.

[2] Clopton Plea Rolls, cit. *CAS* xxxiii. 55 (a man killed with 'a blow of a knife called a thwytel under the right breast'); *Chaucer Life-Records* (1966), p. 357 (a 'thwytyl' used in a brawl, 1381); Cambridgeshire Coroner's Roll, cit. *Documents Relating to Cambridgeshire Villages*, ed. W. M. Palmer and H. W. Saunders (1926) vi. 18 (the son of Walter the plowwright of Trumpington struck John of Girton in the belly with a 'twitel' and killed him).

The lexical value of local documents is still not fully appreciated, as the following instance will show: in an Oxford deed of 1285 Philip the town clerk grants to one John Marshall 'illa domus que dicitur Osthous': the first occurrence of *oasthouse* recorded in *O.E.D.* is 500 years later.

meale'. Lewis took his complaint to the King's Council, who directed that to ensure 'trewe gryndeynge and tollynge of his corne' he should be allowed to bring a miller of his own choosing to grind his corn at the town mill twice a week, and that the bailiffs should pay him in recompense 'aswell of certeyn the said wheate meale so by them [sc. the millers] taken frome him undre pretence of a forfayture as also . . . of suche other corne as the said myllers have stollen frome him, under pretence of tolle, ffower quarters of good wheate meale or els the summe of £4. 13. 4.'.[1]

So what happened to the Cambridge clerks could happen to anybody. But they took not only wheat to Trumpington, they took malt too—'ther was hir whete and eek hir malt ygrounde' (A 3991). Editors never explain why, but college records do. Colleges were large enough institutions to follow the usual monastic practice, and brew their own ale; some still have ale brewed to their own formula. Brewing meant buying malt, or barley for making into malt, which had to be ground before the process could begin. Usually this was done on stones different from those used for grinding wheat: the Trumpington miller may have had a double mill, i.e. two sets of stones—which would make him still more of a power in the land. Brewers, in fact, were as dependent on millers as bakers were—there was a brew-house near the Oxford Castle mill, and a brewery still stands near the site—and as late as 1568 the Oxford Council was enacting that 'wheat malt' was not to be ground 'at any other mill or milles save at the said Castell milles'.[2]

---

[1] *Selections from the Records of the City of Oxford*, ed. W. H. Turner (1880), pp. 179–80 (1546). The custom of taking a proportion of the flour ground as payment survived in Suffolk till the present century. [See also OHS lxxi. 215.]

[2] Ibid., p. 325; cf. p. 338; the conditions of feudalism lasted long after the lord–tenant relation had disappeared. But two years later the Bishop of Oxford leased his half of the mill to a 'Doctor of Philosophy' [*sic*]: OHS xcii. 203. At Durham—a monastery with its own mill to which tenants did suit—the

The mill and its 'services' epitomize the economic and social life of the time. Domesday Book records over 5,000 mills (mostly in the east of England) and the number certainly increased. Hence the elaborate safeguarding of the rights and obligations pertaining to the mill; hence too the attacks on it when unrest came to a head.[1] It was as important to courtier tenant-in-chief as to commoner, and the first readers of the Reeve's Tale, unlike modern critics, would relish the situations they knew in daily life as much as its fabliau-elements. We make something too much—at least musical comedy makes too much—of the earthy humour, just as in the rest of the poetry we make too much of the courtly elegance, or rather, we treat them too distinctly. For every book of Froissart, every poem of Machaut, we should read a set of King's Bench cases, or a Register of the Black Prince or John of Gaunt, which show the flower of England's chivalry playing very practical roles. Chaucer himself spent most of his life not in silken dalliance but making 'rekeninges' (as Clerk of the King's Works he was primarily an accountant), listing pots and pans, checking builders' estimates, travelling, like his Cambridge clerks, along muddy roads.

By the same token, the academic life of his day, though

Master of the Garner received the wheat and malt corn, and noted the amount of malt 'spent' during the week. At Cambridge a malthouse was the last relic of Blackfriars to survive.

Mills for grinding malt as distinct from hard corn are evidenced at least as early as 35 Henry III: cf. the Liberate Rolls for that year, cit. T. Hudson Turner, *Domestic Architecture in England . . . to the End of the Thirteenth Century* (1851), p. 233.

[1] A typical instance of trouble over 'service' is recorded in the *Register of the Black Prince*, ii. 25 ff.: the Prince's mills at Lostwithiel had been misused, and left with broken millstones of local make, and the fishery destroyed; if the burgesses who owe suit to the mill withdraw, the Prince's steward is to constrain them 'by all reasonable means, and also to arrest all the corn and malt (*breys*) which he finds them grinding or taken to be ground at other mills . . . and prevent any strange miller from fetching corn or grain out of the said town to be ground at another's mill'.

it impinged on the court in one direction, in another was
inextricably bound up with rural and manorial concerns.
The masters of the Schools, who as often as not came from
near-by small towns or upland parishes, also ran hostels or,
as bursars, bought or leased farms or tenements, bargained
for stone or timber, supervised harvests, saw to the repair
of mill-spindles or to the purchase of a pick for dressing
millstones. The don of leisured ease was an eighteenth-
century invention. Since everything was done on a shoe-
string, each obolus, each halfpenny of college money had
to be accounted for: whether paid for having the cook's
knife sharpened, or in benefit-money to the said cook
when off work with a 'mormal' on his shin (Chaucer's
Cook suffers from the same affliction), on a shave for the
warden or on 'zedewaude' (the 'cetewale' of the Miller's
Tale) consumed on a jaunt to London, or a warming-
vessel to keep the chaplain's hands warm during Mass in
winter, ointment for a scab, or shoes for a miller's horse or
a fellow's ambling pad. A horse was an important college
investment, as well as a status symbol, and the names of
horses bought and sold are duly recorded. So we know
that in 1300 Merton sold for 13s. 6d. a red horse 'Shyrf
hiȝte'—called Sheriff, as the Reeve's horse is 'highte
Scot' (A 616). The horse in the Reeve's Tale is 'Bayard'
—a name that occurs more than once on Merton Rolls.[1]

To annotate the tales in the light of such records is not
to claim for them Balzacian realism or minute consistency.

[1] All the examples are taken from Dr. R. L. Highfield's edition of *The Early
Rolls of Merton College* (see p. 4, note 1 above); on p. 104 [Bayard] 'stot' has
evidently been misread or miswritten as 'stok': cf. *CT* A 615.

Horses' names deserve study. Several others are given in the Merton Rolls
(e.g. Borel, Wilkin, Favel). They are often double—e.g. Grisel de Suffolk,
Ferant de Burghersh, Grisel Tankarvill, Morel Suffolk, Bayard Lankastre, Dun
de Skelton (*BPR* iv. 34, 66, 71).

('Barillum in quo arma debent mundari', which puzzled Dr. Highfield
(p. 358), doubtless refers to a method of cleaning weapons by rolling them in a
barrel of sand or oil, which is still used in the Metropolitan Museum; cf. *Gawain
and the Green Knight* 2018.)

Accurate description of material objects and *mis en scène* is in itself no great virtue: enough if the poet thereby suggests his setting without tying us to it. And a miscellaneous listening audience called for artistic economy precisely of this kind. It is this economy, more than plot or style or even bawdy incident, that Chaucer learnt from fabliaux. But it follows that when he does flesh his story with detail which is not strictly functional he is not writing at random: he is testifying to the pleasure of particularity. As for the bawdy, to mask it would be to make him false to his time, his genius, and his genre. 'After tea', wrote Dorothy Wordsworth on Boxing Day, 1801, 'we sat by the fire comfortably, and I read aloud the Miller's Tale.' That is the right setting, and the right mood. And a modern audience need not be more squeamish than the Wordsworths.

To reconstruct the milieu of fictional narratives is to risk falling into two traps. The major of these we may call the Macbeth heresy, the minor the Manly heresy. You either extrapolate from the text and regardless of L. C. Knights's warnings indulge in irrelevant inquiries about Lady Macbeth's children, or the Wife of Bath's; or you try to track down 'real-life'—remembering J. M. Manly's devotion to Patent Rolls, we might say 'roll-life'—originals of vividly realized characters; and argue from the alchemy of the Canon's Yeoman's Tale that the poet himself had burnt his fingers, so to speak, on an alembic. So before Professor Northrop Frye accuses me of confusing shapeless stone with finished statue, I must emphasize that I am not, in Chaucer's own phrase, 'a Manly man', and have none of the zeal that prompts devotees of Conan Doyle to refurnish 221 B Baker Street. If I indulge in conjectures it will be simply as a kind of expository shorthand, not because I have a biographical axe to grind. The surmises are not to be pressed home, or taken *au pied de la lettre*, but merely as hints of possibilities hitherto ignored.

At least it may prove refreshing to read a couple of the tales with nothing save Chaucer's first audience in mind; considering not so much how his pilgrims can be supposed to have responded to each other's tales as how his friends would take them, and what they would expect by way of consistency and verisimilitude. In which connection we may recall that when the *Tales* reached print readers in the universities took to them avidly. So published inventories testify, and so we would guess from that reference of Francis Beaumont's to the Cambridge teachers who 'did bring you and me in love with him'.[1]

I speak, then, without any such conviction as moved Samuel Butler to identify Nausicaa's bathing-place, and Kinglake to prove for himself that Neptune, as Homer avers, could have seen the action before Ilium from above Samothrace: 'Now I believed', wrote the author of *Eöthen* after visiting Troy, 'now I *knew*, that this vision of Samothrace overtowering the nearer island [of Imbros] was common to him and to me.' That Chaucer passed along the roads to Oxford and Oseney, to Cambridge and Trumpington, is almost as certain as that Thomas Chaucer was the poet's son; and that Thomas, as sheriff of Oxfordshire, had dealings with Oseney is clear from a reference hitherto overlooked.[2] But I can find nothing to justify Dr. Emden's tentative inclusion of the poet's name amongst Oxford *alumni* (where, to be sure, we also find a

---

[1] Letter to Thomas Speght printed in his edition of Chaucer, 1602. Gabriel Harvey's notes in his copy of this edition show that he was not only in love with Chaucer, he was besotted.

For Cambridge inventories including editions of Chaucer see *CAS* xvi. 181, 188, etc. (Dr. Blythe, Master of the King's Hall, 1541, had both a Chaucer and a Gower); and for a MS. of the *Tales* perhaps associated with Oxford (C.U.L., Dd iv 24) see Manly and Rickert, *The Text of the Canterbury Tales* (1940), i. 105.

[2] OHS xc. 476: a receipt with Thomas Chaucer's official seal for a half-year's rent of Castle Mead and King's Mead, 12 Dec. 1404. Thomas Chaucer 'armiger' also appears as witness to an Oseney document, 10 Nov. 1433 (a year before his death): ibid., p. 400. For other documents indicating his associations with Oxford (and Woodstock) see A. C. Baugh, *PMLA* xlvii (1932), 461–515.

Shakespeare, fellow, and very nearly Warden, of Merton; though he changed his name to Saunders *quia Shakespeare vile reputatum est*). In any case my concern is rather with such questions as: What contact did Chaucer have with academic life? Who shared his scholarly and literary interests? Where would he find those 'autoritees' that he so delighted in?

Of one thing we can be sure: he kept his public constantly before his eyes. The proem to Book Two of *Troilus* even shows him countering objections they might raise to probability. And in interests and sympathies a considerable part of the audience of the *Tales* would fall broadly into the two divisions of Town and Gown—the poles round which his university stories revolve. The Town and Gown division is still with us, but in Chaucer's time and after it was sometimes literally as sharp as a knife—and never more so than in 1381, when the citizens (rather than 'The Peasants') vented their wrath, not without excuse, upon the colleges. Universities, including English universities, have been battle-grounds or trouble-spots for a good part of their history. The tocsin that has lately sounded on many a campus was heard in Oxford some 700 years since, when 'at Seinte Marie churche a clerc þe commun belle rong'—to begin a notable affray. In 1273 fifty Oxford scholars were charged with homicide; and though blood flowed less freely in later centuries, the friction, the horseplay, the rowdyism remained. Academic histories, like academic memoirs, have the curious effect of distancing and embalming the conditions they describe. Thus we are prone to view the whole academic past in the pale violet tints of Andrew Lang's or E. F. Benson's or Sir John Betjeman's anecdotage; forgetting, for instance, that there were riots in Oxford as recently as 1870, and that the tutorial system as we know it had no counterpart in Chaucer's day. It began with Newman and Jowett, and even now shows signs of crumbling.

In Chaucer's day, again, Oxford had little of the prestige that was later to attach to it; and Cambridge had still less. Neither Walter Merton, Chancellor and Bishop of Rochester, nor William Wykeham, Chancellor and Bishop of Winchester, eminent founders of now eminent colleges, had themselves been university men. In range, in volume, in learning, no trio of later poets can match Langland, Gower, and Chaucer; yet apparently not one of them took a degree. The university population—about 1,000 in each town—was drawn largely from religious houses and the poorer classes. In 1358 Oxford, almost certainly followed by Cambridge, claimed that nobles, gentlefolk, and 'very many of the common people' were afraid to send their sons or protégés to university lest the Friars Mendicant there should entice them to enter their order before reaching the years of discretion. Though younger sons of the nobility were beginning to go to Oxford, a London merchant might think it more prudent to send his boy to one of the Inns of Court.[1] The vast majority of undergraduates were *pauperes scholares*—Chaucer's 'poure scoleres'. It is a stock locution, found as early as 1214, when the papal legate decreed that the citizens of Oxford should pay annually fifty-two shillings, with which the abbot of Oseney and the prior of St. Frideswide's should provide a good meal for 100 poor scholars every St. Nicholas's day (the saint was patron of scholars: hence the name of the clerk in the Miller's tale). Such scholars became the regular object of charity. Thus Simon Bredon of Merton (d. 1372) ordered that a residue of his goods should be divided into

---

[1] 'No less than fourteen young nobles' figure among Cambridge petitioners for benefices, 1372–90: E. F. Jacob, *Bulletin of the John Rylands Library*, xxix (1946), 305. Thomas Percy, fifth son of the Baron Percy, was at Queen's in 1351; he became Bishop of Norwich (and a very bad one). Thomas Arundel, third son of the Earl of Arundel, and Gower's patron, was at Oriel *c.* 1370, and became chancellor of the university, and Archbishop. When the sons of the Marquis of Dorset went up in 1494, the university officially welcomed them with wine and wafers: OHS lxxiii. 353.

three parts, one for the needy, one for dowries for honest girls, and one for poor scholars. More touching is the bequest of Bishop Grandison of Exeter, of a commentary on Saint Augustine 'to some poor Oxford scholar studying theology'; if this scholar dies or obtains office, it is to be passed on to others in like case, and kept at Merton for this purpose for ever; and at Merton it still is.[1] It was just such a clerk as Chaucer's, not 'so worldly for to have office', that Grandison had in mind.

Pauperes scholares, we shall see, were not necessarily destitute. But that they were a recognizable type is clear from Chaucer's contrast of the friar's semi-cope of double worsted, and the threadbare coat of his clerk (A 260–2). The Ellesmere artist ignores this hint, depicting the clerk in lay cloak and hood, and carrying a clasped book bound in red in either hand—an allusion to his ruling passion rather than a realistic portrait of a travelling scholar.[2] Yet he *may* have carried to Canterbury a portable breviary, so that he could 'for the soules preye / Of hem that yaf hym wherwith to scoleye' (A 301–2)—a phrase that would cover benefactors direct or indirect.[3] At Merton twelve 'poor secondary scholars' (besides three chaplains) were paid to sing for the souls of benefactors of the founder. It was concern for the welfare of souls (as the name of a famous Oxford college should remind us) that prompted all the early foundations. Hence Walter de Merton's

---

[1] It is now Merton MS. E. 1. 6: see F. M. Powicke, *The Medieval Books of Merton College* (1931), p. 137. For Bredon see ibid., p. 85, and p. 59 below. For 'poor scholars' see Appendix A.

[2] In fact, 'clad in blak or reed' (*CT* A 294) probably indicates that he was indifferent to binding: if the list of books for sale by J. Dorne a century or so later is any guide, many ordinary books were sold in quires or parchment covers: see Strickland Gibson, *Early Oxford Bindings* (1903). By the turn of the fourteenth century the usual colour of Oxford bindings was white.

[3] By the same token, readers of books bought with money given by benefactors and then bequeathed to a college are enjoined to pray for both benefactor and donor: cf. Powicke, op. cit., p. 171, and M. R. James, *A Descriptive Catalogue of the Manuscripts in the Library of Peterhouse* (1899), p. 36.

statement of intent: '. . . ipsamque Domum, pro salute anime mee et animarum prefati domini regis Anglie, Ricardi regis Romanorum . . . necnon parentum et bene-factorum meorum omnium . . . ex abundanti fundo et stabilio . . .'[1] Chaucer's clerk 'unto logyk hadde longe ygo' (A 286), i.e. he has possibly already been a Regent Master, though he was still supported by his 'freendes' (299). So too the dreamer in *Piers Plowman*, in a passage that curiously anticipates Chaucer's lines, says:

> When ich yonge was, meny 3er hennes,
> My fader and my frendes founden me to scole
> Til ich wiste wyterliche what holi wryt menede
>
> (C. vi. 35–7)

—where 'frendes' probably means 'family', 'scole' univer-sity, and the last line may imply reading in theology. He goes on to indicate that the death of his 'frendes' cut short his studies; which would be nothing unusual—few stayed the whole long course. The Wife of Bath's fifth husband, Jankin, whom she married 'for love, and no richesse', cer-tainly did not:

> He *somtyme* was a clerk of Oxenford
> And hadde left scole, and went at home to bord.
>
> (D 527–8)

Jankin was barely twenty, so can hardly have reached his regency, which would have qualified him for a higher post than that of parish clerk. But, as Chaucer indicates (A 291), not all graduates could get benefices, despite constant efforts of the university to provide them, whilst college fellowships were few, impermanent, and far from lucrative: papal permission to hold one along with a small benefice was sometimes granted on grounds of poverty.

Why, we may ask at this point, does Chaucer associate his pilgrim clerk (and others) so firmly with Oxford? First

---

[1] Founder's Statutes as printed in OHS N.S. xviii. 379.

(leaving aside any possible personal reasons for the prefer-
ence), because the chances were overwhelmingly in favour
of a clerk's being an Oxford man. Emden's Oxford *Biographical Register* contains about four times as many entries
as his Cambridge volume—which means, incidentally,
that Chaucer could count on far more Oxford readers than
Cambridge ones. Secondly, an Oxford scholar setting out
on pilgrimage would be likely to make for Saint Thomas's
shrine. Oxford had a parish of St. Thomas, a St. Thomas
Hall, a fraternity of St. Thomas with a private chapel at
St. Mary's, the university church, and an annual gathering
for Mass on St. Thomas's day, followed by a dinner; the
fraternity's chantry priest, who acted as gospeller to the
vicar of the parish, said Mass daily between five and six
a.m., so that travellers and scholars could attend before
beginning their day.[1] An Oxford man, then, might well
have a special devotion to St. Thomas; and the Oxford
carpenter and his wife both swear by him. Again, Oxford
had supplied several primates to Canterbury, one of whom,
Edmund of Abingdon, had been canonized and had two
Oxford halls named after him. To a Mertonian, moreover
(and we shall see that Chaucer had connections with Merton), the Canterbury journey would provide an opportunity to pray before the tomb of the founder of his house,
at Rochester. Finally, it was easy to get from Oxford to
Southwark, where the pilgrimage began. A Cambridge
man, on the other hand, would more naturally go to
Walsingham, England's next most popular shrine, in
near-by Norfolk. This is exactly what Erasmus did, when
staying in Cambridge. In May 1512 he rode the seventy
miles to Walsingham with a young fellow of King's called
Robert Aldrich, who was to become headmaster and
provost of Eton (the twin foundation to King's) and

---

[1] OHS c. 129; lxxxv. 150–1; for St. Thomas Hall see ibid., 186. For the
prayers used at the *Memoria* of St. Thomas see OHS lvi. xxiii. The saint
figured on the seal of Canterbury Hall: see OHS lxiv. 161.

Bishop of Carlisle.[1] Erasmus's Dialogue, *A Pilgrimage for Religion's Sake*, is in some sort a sceptical Cambridge counterpart to Chaucer's Prologue.

Of scepticism, even of Ockhamite scepticism, there is little trace in Chaucer. The doctor whose study 'was but litel on the Bible' was at most a Laodicean. That he had studied medicine at Oxford we are nowhere told; but the learning that Chaucer credits him with he could easily have absorbed there. Few physicians can have had their own copies of all the works he knew (A 429–34), and in fact I can find no record of any collection containing them except Merton College Library. There lay the *Aphorisms* of 'olde Ypocras' (in Constantinus's translation from the Arabic); the same 'Constantin's' *Pantegni* ($\Pi\alpha\nu\tau\epsilon\chi\nu\acute{\eta}$); Galen (probably the *Ars Parva*, or *Tegni* ($\tau\epsilon\chi\nu\acute{\eta}$); the *Liber Messue* of Chaucer's Damascenus; the *Compendium Medicinae* of 'Gilbertin', Gilbertus Anglicus; the *Lilium Medicinae* by Bernard of Gordon; 'Razis' (Abu Bakr al-Razi, the greatest clinician of the Middle Ages); Ali ibn abī al-Rijāl's *De Judiciis Astrorum* (Chaucer's 'Haly'); Averroes (the *Liber Universalis*, or *Colliget*); the *Canon* of Avicenna (Merton has one of the finest copies of this great work); and the *Liber Aggregatus* of Chaucer's Serapion— an alphabetical arrangement of Galen and Dioscorides— was summarized in a Merton manuscript now lost (381). Chaucer's 'Rufus' is the only text not now to be found in the Merton catalogues; but we do find among the medical texts the works of Arnauld of Villeneuve, the 'Arnold of the Newe toune' cited by the Canon's yeoman, and a *geomancia*: the kind of book that provided the figures of Puella and Rubeus mentioned in the Knight's Tale. Moreover Merton men (and their contemporaries) went to lectures on Aristotle 'de inspiracione et respiracione, de sensu et sensato'. From notes of such lectures, or from the

---

[1] *Erasmi Epistolae*, ed. P. S. Allen (1906), i. 513. The road ran by Barton Mills, Brandon, and Swaffham, and part of it is still called the Pilgrims' Way.

texts just cited, Chaucer could have picked up the array of technical terms that the Knight uses to describe Arcite's 'maladye of hereos', and his dissolution. The lectures on Aristotle 'de somno et vigilia' (a prescribed text from 1340) would likewise have appealed to a poet so much concerned with sleep and dream.[1]

Only two of the physician's authorities, Gilbertus and Gaddesden, were Englishmen, and John Gaddesden, the most eminent physician and medical writer of the century, was also the first of an illustrious line of Merton medicos. A fellow by 1307, he did not proceed Doctor of Medicine till c. 1332, when he was rector of Chipping Norton. His massive *Rosa Medicinae* earned him a gold rose from the Black Prince, in whose Register the gift is duly noted (and it probably took its name from that rose).[2] Merton had two copies of it, both given by fellows, and one of them bears the names of three Merton men in jottings which show that they were born in streets Chaucer walked in daily: Blanchpayn and Stonham 'in Milkstrete, *nati* London in Chepe', and Scardeburgh 'in strata seu vico vulgariter nuncupato Lombarde Strete'. Blanchpayn was an exact contemporary of Chaucer: fellow from 1359 to 1380 or later, sub-warden 1369–70, and present at the famous council called at Blackfriars, London, to condemn a Merton man, John Wiclif. Robert Stonham was fellow by

---

[1] For the Merton MSS. referred to see Powicke, op. cit., index. Several of these titles are not to be found in the largest known collections of medical MSS.— St. Augustine's and Christ Church, Canterbury (for which see R. H. Robbins in *Studies in Honor of Margaret Schlauch*, Warsaw, 1966). The list of medical works in the Cambridge University Library c. 1424 (see H. Bradshaw, *CAS* xiii (1863), 253) does not include Gaddesden or Gilbertus or the *Pantegni*. *De somno et vigilia*, of course, was a common text.

[2] *BPR* iv. 69. Another standard medical text, John Mirfield's *Breviarium Bartolomaei*, has Oxford connections: one copy was prepared for the hospital at Abingdon, and another, now at Pembroke College, Oxford, has prefixed an astronomical calendar prepared in 1380 by Friar John Somer, of the kind associated with Oxford: see pp. 75–6 below. The *Breviarium* includes some lively stories such as Chaucer would have relished.

A fellow of Merton, T. Goulston, was to edit Galen in the 17th century.

1384, sub-warden in 1396–7. When he died whilst attending the Council of Pisa (such men got about), he had with him Wiclif's reply to *quaestiones* put to him by yet another Merton man, Chaucer's 'philosophical Strode'.

That Chaucer should include in the *dramatis personae* of the Tales no fewer than five academics—not to mention the Franklin's 'clerk of Orleans' or the Friar's allusion to 'scole matere' (D 1272)—is itself remarkable. It is still more remarkable that the two tales of student life are the only tales in the whole canon that are so firmly tied to a local setting; and that setting is made part of the very texture of the stories told by two of the most vividly drawn of all his narrators. The other tales of Canterbury are for the most part tales of Greece, Syria, Brittany, Flanders, Rome. Chaucer the Londoner tells us little about London, and the loquacious goodwife of Bath tells us nothing about Bath. The poet chose to set some of his most domestic scenes in the two university towns; and not a detail in them can be faulted.

In fact Chaucer the Londoner was for most of his life servant of kings who were still perambulating monarchs, living off their estates. Edward and Richard regularly held court at the great palace of Woodstock, eight miles to the north of Oxford and reached, from London, only through Oxford (where so many good roads converged). The first occurrence of Chaucer's name is in household accounts drawn up at Woodstock in 1357, three years before he travelled from Canterbury with Lionel of Ulster via Boughton-under-Blee, Ospringe, Sittingbourne, Rochester, and Dartford, the places that were to figure so much later in his Tales. The royal interest in Oxford had been signalized by the gift of the manor of Beaumont, just outside its walls, to the Carmelite friars who are commemorated by Friars' Entry (opposite St. Mary Magdalen church), and friars associated with Oxford houses kept the spiritual secrets of king and queen for several reigns. Queen Philippa took a lively concern in the college founded in 1340 by her chaplain and in her honour, and Edward III befriended the royal foundation of Oriel. Increasingly Westminster looked to the universities for its civil servants, and by 1370 Langland was complaining that B.A.s and M.A.s and even doctors in orders 'serven the kyng and his silver tellen, / In Cheker and in Chancerye chalengen his dettes' (*Piers Plowman*, Prol. B 92–3). It was one of the functions of the King's Hall at Cambridge —a royal fundation that will come into our story—to provide a supply of such men, who, as celibates, were conveniently movable at short notice. The founder of the greatest fourteenth-century college, William of Wykeham, who had himself begun life as a civil servant, would be conscious of the need, and opportunities, for trained men.[1]

Not only are our two tales tied to these university localities, they are bound to each other in a tight warp and woof of parallels and contrasts, verbal echoes and reflections. It is not merely a matter of antagonism in the characters and callings of the two narrators or of the shared motifs of the cuckolding clerk and snoring husband, things mis-seen in the dark, bourgeois wives on parade at church, or of descriptions in one tale recalling images or phrases in the other: as when Jankin's 'swete note' is counterpointed by the 'stif burdoun' of the sleeping miller's snores, which provide the crude Cambridge compline (A 4171) to balance the Oxford lauds (A 3655) —or the colt's 'wehee' echoes Alison's 'teehee' (with Alison Nicholas can 'rage and play', but none 'dorste rage or ones pleye' with Simkin's wife). Even the oaths and the furnishings are similar: 'Seint Thomas' and 'Seint Frideswide' are simply replaced as expletives by 'Seint Cutberd'

---

[1] They would find that knowledge of *dictamen* was an asset. For the connection of extant dictaminal treatises with Oxford see R. S. Schoeck, *Medieval Studies*, xxx (1968), 214–25. Cf. p. 82 below

and 'Rood of Bromeholm'; beds and beards and headdress and the lubricant of ale figure in both stories; and in both descriptive phrases are nicely weighted: 'hende' giving just the same value to Nicholas's *courtoisie* as 'ycomen of noble kin' does to the rank of a priest's illegitimate daughter. Controlling both narratives is the theme of clerkly cunning, the 'sleightes of philosophye' pitted against plain men's practice. Nicholas, who had 'lerned art', first shows that he is a clerk 'ful subtile and ful queynte' (A 3275) by his play with Alison; the miller twits the Cambridge clerks who had 'lerned art', after they had shown a conspicuous lack of ordinary prudence. It is as if the Reeve (whose 'prologue' is an essential link as well as a revealing gloss) had taken note of every phrase in the tale told against a member of his own mystery and turned it to profit—just as he was wont to 'yeve and lene' to his master goods that were not his to give and lend, and yet get credit for so doing (A 609–12).

Is it fanciful to see in this distorted-mirror effect evidence that the two tales were meant to be read as one? Certainly the towns and universities in which they are set resembled each other more closely in Chaucer's time than they have ever done since. The urban and academic nomenclature of both was identical, and extant records for the one place can elucidate bare references in the other. Thus 'Glomery Hall' bulks large in early Cambridge history, so that we can infer from it the functions of Merton's *magister glomerie* and of the Oxford regent masters appointed to supervise the teaching of grammar.[1] 'Swans nest' is merely a name on Cambridge maps, but we know that at Oxford the city kept swans in a similar location, and made profit from them.[2] Both towns stood at

---

[1] See OHS lxxiii. 278 and lxxxix. 216. Oseney Abbey sent pupils to a grammar school (ibid., p. 218). It is not inconceivable that 'litel Lowys' was at such a school: see p. 22 n. 2.

[2] *Oxoniensia,* xxxi. 74. Christ Church took careful count of its swans and cygnets up and down the river: OHS xcii. 195.

strategic river crossings and the river played an essential part in the life of each. On both rivers stood a King's Mill, and a hythe (though only Oxford now preserves that term). 'Small' (i.e. narrow) bridges and a 'Great Bridge' crossed the Cam, and bridges with the same names the streams of the Thames. Both towns were overlooked by a formidable castle, and surrounded by a gated wall or ditch, with suburbs creeping out beyond. Both, finally, were low-lying, and thus subject to pestilence. If the Oxford schools had been built on Headington Hill, or the Cambridge schools on the Gogs, Max Beerbohm might not have poeticized the Oxford miasma, nor Milton the Cambridge sedge, but the whole intellectual history of England might have been different. River valleys (witness Eton and Winchester) have their own distinctive intellectual 'climate'.

It did indeed seem possible to Walter de Merton—and even to Robert Eaglesfield, founder of Queen's in Chaucer's lifetime—that the university might remove from Oxford; and the migration to Stamford in 1333, though abortive, long left its traces on the Statutes. But the future of both places as seats of learning had been assured as soon as the friars built their Schools. At Cambridge these were at first on the wrong side of the river, but the track to Newnham proved so miry in winter—Oxonians latinized Cambridge as Lutetia, the place of mud—that they moved within the town ditch (piping their water all the way from Madingley, just as the canons of Oseney brought theirs from Hinksey Hill). At Cambridge hardly a stone of a religious house remains *in situ*, though one is built into the walls of the new Blackfriars, outside the city. At Oxford the demolitions at St. Ebbe's have lately revealed the footings of the Greyfriars church just beyond the city wall, which formed the north wall of the choir; the building was some 300 feet long and 40 feet wide with a narrower chancel at the east end, and the district is still known as The Friars.[1] There were about a hundred Friars Minor and seventy Preachers in Oxford in Chaucer's time; and he is recognizing the friars' part in the life of the town when he punctuates the Miller's tale by their bells, which tell Nicholas it is time to rise, as 'freres in the chauncel gonne synge' (3656); it is still dark, so they would be singing matins or lauds.

Their role in the Schools was the more important in that Oxford and Cambridge were the only universities outside Paris that could grant degrees in theology. For the friars produced most of the masters in that subject; and when most students, like Nicholas, lived perforce in lodgings, the friars could offer board, free tuition, and the use of good libraries to anyone over fourteen, the normal age of entrance to the universities.[2] The disputations leading to the Oxford M.A. degree were originally held at the Augustinian convent outside Smithgate, and 'doing Austins' remained the term for these exercises long after that site was occupied by Wadham College. At Cambridge the friars had three separate libraries; and Archbishop Fitzralph, sometime Chancellor of Oxford, complained that friars bought up all the books used in medicine and civil law, as well as those used in canon law, arts, and theology. It was not only poverty that made it hard for Chaucer's clerk to buy his texts of Aristotle.

The academic concern, or jealousy, that lies behind Fitzralph's complaint also lies behind much of anti-Mendicant polemic and satire in fabliau, and in Chaucer; which is not always to be taken at its face value. In the Summoner's Tale the friar protests to the lord that an 'old churl' has done despite to him:

---

[1] See now *Oxoniensia*, xxxvi (1971), 6–8.

[2] In 1386 both universities petitioned Parliament to raise the minimum age to sixteen. If this was the usual age by the time Chaucer wrote the *Astrolabe* (1391) the 'litel Lowys' to whom it is addressed can scarcely have been an undergraduate.

'Now maister,' quod this lord, 'I yow biseke,—'
'No *maister*, sire,' quod he, 'but *servitour*;
Thogh I have had in scole swich honour,
God liketh nat that "Raby" men us calle—'   (D 2184–7)

He means that he has indeed taught theology at the university (a few lines later he trots out the academic tag *per
consequens*), but that he disowns the worldly title *magister*,
citing the very text which the Paris masters had used as an
argument that their rivals, the Friars Preachers, ought not
to teach in the Schools, where they would have to take this
title of Master.[1] Some of this hostility seeps into the
theological arguments of Wiclif, the great Oxford master
of Chaucer's day; and some of the Oxford sympathy for
Wiclif's cause had the same source.

But in practice friars and academics rubbed along rather
better than the polemics of the time might suggest. Certainly the founding fellows of Merton were on friendly
enough terms with the religious orders. Walter de Merton
himself left money to the Oxford Friars Minor; and his
colleagues consulted an Oxford friar called Thomas about
the building of its chapel, just after the Augustinians had
finished building theirs (with the help of timber sent by
Henry III from Woodstock). From time to time the college gave gifts of wine to the friars, and once bought some
parchment 'ad opus fratris Willelmi de Sotebroke de
ordine minorum'—for what purpose we know not.[2] William of Wykeham left a shilling to every friar in Oxford—
which meant 279 shillings; Salter thought that rather less
than a third of these would be university men. With the
citizenry, too, the friars must have been on good terms.
One third of all known Oxford wills of the fourteenth
century contain bequests to the Friars Minor; and a Carmelite confraternity flourished at Cambridge.

But there were monks at Oxford long before there were

[1] Cf. N. F. Rigolado, *Poetic Patterns in Ruteboeuf* (Yale, 1970), p. 176 n. 78.
[2] OHS N.S. xviii. 295; also pp. 293, 304.

friars. It was first of all the city of Saint Frideswide (and
of Saint Frideswide's fair). Her feast figured in all calendars (and her Mass in one text of the Sarum missal), so
that readers would at once perceive why John the Oxford
carpenter invokes her (*CT* A 3449). In the fourteenth
century, however, it was not Saint Frideswide's monastery
with its noble Norman tower so much as the towers and
spires of Oseney Abbey, just beyond the Castle—the kind
of site always favoured by Augustinian Canons—that
would catch a traveller's eye: a vast array of buildings, of
which only a doorway now remains, though Dr. Johnson
and Tom Warton (that early connoisseur of the Gothic)
found enough to leave the Doctor speechless with indigna-
tion at the ruined glory. But the Abbey had been maintained by revenues drawn from a hundred or so tenements
within the town and owned by or bequeathed to the
Canons. Oseney has its place in Chaucer's Oxford tale
because of its place in the Oxford of its time, when colleges
in the modern sense scarcely existed, and the very term
'college' was a rarity. In the Oxford colleges as we know
them, only Merton's Mob Quad gives us a genuine sense
of Chaucer's century. The tower and cloister of the College of Saint Mary of Winton, the 'new' college of his
time, were still building as he wrote; and Bohemian
sculptors—brought over, Professor Pächt believes, by the
Queen to whom Chaucer pays compliment in *Troilus*—
were still fashioning details of its chapel 'after the newe
guise of Beaume', in Gower's phrase. The scholars of the
new foundation were few enough for the warden (like the
provost of Queen's) to be able to observe their goings out
and their comings in from his lodgings over the college
gates; a position much resembling that of Chaucer's
mansio over Aldgate. At Cambridge only the back court
of Corpus survives unscathed from that time. 'Pythagoras
Hall', lately scraped and garnished, is to be sure of earlier
date, but despite its name it was never an academic hall:

it was a little piece of Merton in Cambridge, and as such will come into our story. It is the very absence of collegiate life and institutions as we know them that made possible the antics of 'hende Nicholas', as Chaucer's miller described them. To these I shall next turn.

II

TOWN AND GOWN

My title is irresistible, for Chaucer himself, at the very opening of the Miller's Tale, makes a juxtaposition that is not to be found in any of the analogues. In these—and they are all later than the tale—the husband, a carpenter or rich merchant, is cuckolded by a friar, a miller, or a priest, not by a student. Chaucer's carpenter is 'a riche gnoffe', but his naïvety suggests that he does not belong to the oligarchy of wealthy merchants who (says Dr. Pantin) ran Oxford, as they ran other medieval towns, and who resented the presence of the university. The term 'gnoffe', like its cognates, carries a derogatory sense, as witnessed by the next occurrence, in Drant's *Horace* (1566): 'the chubbishe gnof that toyles and moyles'. There is a hint in John the carpenter of Snug the Joiner. In 1610 Healey uses Chaucer's phrase to translate Saint Augustine's contemptuous *crassis divitibus*, 'the crass rich' (*De Civitate Dei* xiv. iv. 501).

Carpenters were numerous in medieval Oxford, and thanks to college account rolls and Mr. E. A. Gee we know the names and activities of some twenty who were working there between 1370 and 1400.[1] The craft may include joiners, woodcarvers, sawyers, even foresters who cut down trees. The carpenter was as important as the mason, for most houses (as distinct from colleges) were built at least partly of wood, and most fittings were wood.[2]

---

[1] *Oxoniensia*, xvii (1952), 112–84. Carpenters are also often named in records of the preceding century.

[2] Tackley Inn, which still stands (though disguised) in the High Street, was one of the few houses built mainly of stone; but it was built as an investment by

[*cont. on p. 29*]

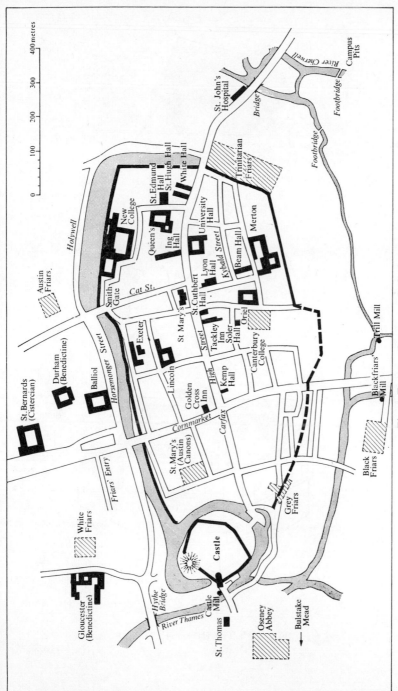

Fig. 1 Fourteenth-century Oxford

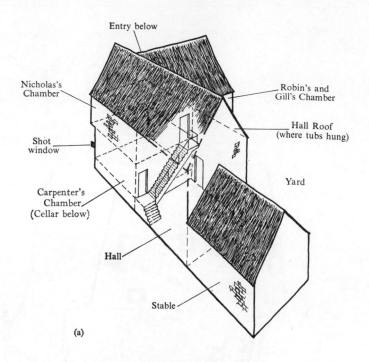

Entry below

Nicholas's Chamber

Robin's and Gill's Chamber

Hall Roof (where tubs hung)

Shot window

Yard

Carpenter's Chamber (Cellar below)

Hall

Stable

(a)

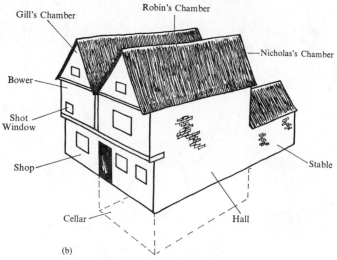

Gill's Chamber

Robin's Chamber

Nicholas's Chamber

Bower

Shot Window

Shop

Stable

Cellar

Hall

(b)

Fig. 2a, b The Carpenter's House

But not much house-building went on in the years following the Black Death, when in the very centre of Oxford
there was vacant land available for lease as a garden.[1] A
carpenter was more likely to find work in, or for, one of
the abbeys or one of the new colleges. In the seventies, for
instance, Merton was building a fine library, for which a
carpenter called Robert provided much of the woodwork
by contract; and it is a sign of the status which a member
of the mystery might attain that two of them dined in hall
whilst working at New College,[2] and one of these was
portrayed in glass at Winchester College. It is largely on
college accounts that Thorold Rogers based his tables of
carpenters' wages: a good workman could earn a shilling
a day, as against the fourpence laid down by the Statute of
Labourers, and two Merton carpenters, Thomas Bloxham
and 'Nicholas', were in 1390 fined under that statute for
taking too much pay. An able master-craftsman would be
offered work outside his own town—like Hugh Harland,
whom Bishop Wykeham employed at both Oxford and
Winchester. Wykeham was Clerk of the King's Works
some years before Chaucer; and his dealings with Harland
suggest that one of the Clerk's duties was to supervise
the work of the King's chief carpenter—for such Harland had been.[3] His name occurs along with those of
Geoffrey and Philippa Chaucer in the list of allowances
for mourning to be worn at Queen Philippa's funeral in
1369, when Harland and one John Massyngham figure
as 'valletz de mistere'. Harland's son (it seems) went

Roger le Mareschal, vicar of Tackley, as an academic inn; see W. A. Pantin,
'The development of domestic architecture in Oxford', *The Antiquaries Journal*,
xxvii (1947), 127.

[1] *Register of Godstow Nunnery*, ii (EETS o.s. 130, 1906), p. 493. But one
Peter, a carpenter, built a new house *c.* 1370: *Oxoniensia*, xvii. 159.

[2] The earliest Hall Book of New College records that Henry Yevele, Hugh
Harland, and Wm. Wynford dined in the 26th week of the year 1388.

[3] With Yevele, he was responsible for the transformation of Westminster Hall:
see H. M. Colvin, *The History of the King's Works* (1964), i. 529.

up to the college his father had helped to build, about 1397.[1]

A further indication of John's status must be noticed. He can afford both a serving boy or apprentice (Robin), for himself, and a maid (Gill) for his wife;[2] and he can plausibly get them out of the way by sending them to London on an errand, so he may have had craft connections with that city as Harland did. They would travel on horseback—why should he have a stable in his garden (A 3572) if not to keep a horse or two?—but even so would take at least two days each way, making the journey (probably in company) by the usual stages: Tetsworth, High Wycombe, Uxbridge.[3] John himself, if not 'wise' or 'shaply' enough to be an alderman (like the carpenter who jostles with the haberdasher in the Prologue (361–72)), evidently had enough 'catel' and 'rente' to have made the Canterbury journey, and on his own horse.

John makes his own ladders for climbing up to his tubs. Ladders were costly: a carpenter called Robert sold one to Merton in 1377 for 3s. 2d. (a week's wages). But he has no kimlins of his own, though carpenters often made similar objects—like orchard troughs, or lids for troughs (*albeis*); *una pipa ad conservandos panes* (a big breadbox) was made for Magdalen in 1474 by John Carow, a fine craftsman, some of whose work survives. Our John seems to spend most of his time at Oseney, where he was a familiar figure (A 3664); since he could have been sent off to the abbey's grange for timber he must have been thought competent and reliable (3666 ff.).

---

[1] Soon afterwards the son of an Oxford town clerk came up from Winchester; forty years later he was chancellor of the university. The tragedy of Jude the Obscure was played more often in the nineteenth century than in the fourteenth.

[2] For Oxford citizens with one or more *servientes* of either sex see, for example, lxxiii. 101.

[3] If John hired a post-horse it might take three days: hostelries kept such horses on Port Meadow, where they were grass-fed (and so not expected to travel fast).

John is rich enough to attract a pretty wife and to own a commodious house, called indifferently a hostelry or 'inn' (3203, 3622); both terms imply that it was large enough to be rented as an academic hall or a grammar hall—for houses were taken for such purposes by the year; most halls were originally private houses, as the name Peter-*house* reminds us. But he is rather mean, at least unwilling to let a spare room go to waste. So he boards the 'hende' Nicholas, who 'had lerned art'—i.e. was probably Bachelor of Arts—but was now crazy about astrology. The Miller's description of Nicholas as 'poor', if not purely conventional, must be ironic. He is not too poor to have a room to himself or a shelf full of books 'greet and small' (including an *Almagest*, the Merton copy of which, *cum multis aliis in uno magno volumine*, had cost seven shillings); and he owned a psaltery, and an astrolabe. To sing *Angelus ad virginem* was simply to follow collegiate custom of singing the Antiphon to the Virgin after compline or the evening collation. But there is evidently other music at night as well.

> And thus this sweete clerk his tyme spente
> After *his freendes* fyndyng, and his rente.   (3219–20)

Unlike the ideal student of the Prologue, he is squandering the money his family had collected to 'put him through college'. It all has a familiar ring, and indeed echoes Deschamps's complaints about the way some students spent their time (*Miroir de Mariage* 2081–9). If 'rent' has its modern sense we should bear in mind that the price of lodgings was probably the same as that of *camerae* ('chambers') in academic halls, which was fixed by *taxatores*, assessors chosen from the owners and the university to decide on a fair charge: it might range from 20*s*. to 5*s*. p.a.[1]

---

[1] See OHS c. 103, lxx. 29, and Emden, *An Oxford Hall* (1927), p. 118. The phrase 'at board' (cf. 3188) is not recorded in *O.E.D.* before 1688, but it occurs in the Cambridge Poll Tax returns for 1512: they list four men who were 'atte borde' with one Robert Cobbe (*Cambridge Borough Documents*, i, ed. W. M. Palmer (1931), p. 122).

But 'rent' probably here means income; which would imply that he had some money from other sources. Merton once had an arrangement by which a man in lodgings *in villa*—in the town—was given a sum in lieu of commons. Nicholas would evidently spend all the £4 per annum for books and £5 for clothes that in 1335 a father was ordered to provide for his son's maintenance at the university. At a time when undergraduates lived on 5*d*. a week, a text of Aristotle's *Physics* (*et al.*) cost £1. 6*s*. 8*d*., a commentary thereon £1. 4*s*. 0*d*., and the *De Animalibus* ('bound in red') £1. But some short texts were as low as 6*d*.[1]

Chaucer's lines provide much the fullest inventory of a scholar's belongings before the sixteenth century. 'Belongings' would probably include 'his presse ycovered with a faldying reed' (3212): the earliest actual inventories extant (dated 1438 and later) sometimes include a desk (*lectrinum*) —the absence of which from Chaucer's list may be significant—and often a musical instrument—a lute or psaltery, as here. One includes a standing press with boards— evidently bookshelves. Nicholas keeps his books where the clerk of the Prologue kept them—at his bed's head; if John of Salisbury is to be trusted, this was monastic custom (*Policraticus* vii. 19). I do not find shelves in such a position depicted in interiors of the period; and the *Book of the Duchess* (46–8) indicates that Chaucer kept his books elsewhere. But the Liberate Rolls of Henry III include an order for 'a wide table to be put at the head of the king's bed'.[2] Perhaps Nicholas had such a table, and used his

[1] For comparative costs see H. E. Salter, in *Essays in History Presented to R. L. Poole* (1927), pp. 422 ff. A fellow of Merton could probably have afforded to buy a few books out of his personal allowance of £50.

[2] Cit. T. Hudson Turner, *Domestic Architecture in England . . . to the End of the Thirteenth Century* (1851), p. 232. A 'frame of oke' for books is mentioned in an inventory of 1598 ptd. Bradshaw: *CAS* iii. 186; cf. *Life-Records of Chaucer*, ed. F. J. Furnivall, ii (1876), p. xvii. The poet of the *Kingis Quair* when he has finished reading his *Boece* in bed, puts it 'at my hede' (l. 52). For an inventory of a Merton fellow's rooms in 1509 see OHS lxxvi. 397; the only books men-

press solely to keep his clothes in. He sweetens the air by
hanging bunches of herbs about the room—a desirable
deodorizer if a neighbour kept pigs or threw his stockfish
water into the street. Robert Burton will remark that
juniper 'is in great request with us at Oxford, to sweeten
our chambers'.

The most notable item among this clerk's possessions
is the astrolabe. Even the fellows of Merton had at this
time only three between them; and it was one of the great
advantages of being a fellow that you could borrow such
things for a whole year at the annual *electio* of distribution
of books. Chaucer, to be sure, indicates that he bought an
astrolabe to give to his 'little Lewis' before he had learnt
much Latin.[1] But 'Lewis' may be a fiction, to justify the
simplicity with which the poet describes '*a certein noumbre
of conclusiouns* aperteining to the same instrument'. The
phrase is the very same that defines Nicholas's degree of
astronomical knowledge (3193). With the help of his
augrim stones, or *lapis calculatoria* (Merton had only one
set of these), Nicholas, like Lewis, could probably work
out the 'verrey degree of any maner starre', the altitude of
planets, and so forth; Chaucer himself always links rain-
storms with the planets—as in the lines to Scogan (sometimes called an Oxford man, which we should expect the
tutor of Henry IV's sons to be):

> But now so wepith Venus in hir spere
> That with hir teeres she wol drenche us here

—in stanzas that with their reference to the 'worde eterne'
and 'statutz hye in hevene' recall the fateful 'smoky reyn'
associated with 'influences of thise hevenes hye' in *Troilus*
iii. 617 ff. But Nicholas can work out only '*a certeyn* of

tioned are thirty-three works in theology out of the college library; see OHS
N.S. vi. 80–95 for some revealing lists of the same period.

[1] This may have been a 'mini': some are only a few inches in diameter. For
recent accounts of the astrolabe see *Cahiers de civilisation médiévale*, lvii (1972),
28. For (unofficial) study of astronomy at the universities see ibid. 36.

conclusiouns'—a limited number; he is of strictly amateur status.

Nicholas has a room to himself 'withouten any compaignye' (the Miller borrows that phrase from the Knight's Tale to emphasize the point). He is thus more comfortably off than a student living in an academic hall, where men 'chummed' with a senior or, as in the Benedictine hostel at Cambridge, shared a common bedroom which had three or four small studies opening off it. In the phrase of the period, he is a 'chambredekyn', which Antony Wood derived from *in camera degentes*, 'students living in digs'. In 1413 mendicant Irish 'chambredekyns' were expelled the country; and in an Oxford statute of *c.* 1410 'chambredekyns' *nephando nomine* are said to sleep by day and haunt taverns by night; a charge echoed a century later in the complaint that they 'kepe themselfe in their chambre from mornynge tyll nyghte for to be seen vertuous fellowes, but never the lesse when it is nyght they wyll rushe out in harnesse [with weapons] into the stretes like as foxis doth out of their holys'.

As early as 1313, the chief occupant of any house with clerks living in it had been required to report any improper behaviour to the Chancellor or proctors. But it is a difficult matter to keep Nicholases under surveillance; Gower's fling at the *clerus* who studies to write the laws of Nature in his own way (*in arte sua*: *Vox Clamantis* III. xvii) had some grounds; and it was precisely because of such goings-on as enliven our tale that the university decreed that in future all scholars should reside in a Hall or College where commons are kept 'or in halls annexed to the same, or should battel with the same' or be liable to be cut off by expulsion 'like a rotten limb'.[1] So it is to Nicholas and his

---

[1] *Statuta Antiqua*, ed. Strickland Gibson (1931), p. 208. Residence within college walls did not of course completely cure the evil. For a fellow who consorted with women and nightwalkers, frequented taverns till 10 p.m., and sometimes even slept out of college, see OHS lxxxv. 47 ff.

kind that we indirectly owe the establishment of the collegiate system. For though in his time there were eight
colleges, they were essentially small graduate societies.
The halls were far more numerous, but unendowed and
impermanent, and probably reluctant to do more than
provide a few lectures for some ten to thirty scholars who
shared a common table. St. Edmund Hall preserves the
name, and till this century kept the status, of such an
institution; and there is still a Beam Hall in Merton
Street—once, like many others, an Oseney property.
Academic inns—*hospicia*—as distinct from halls (*aulae* or
domus) were less common;[1] they were commodious houses
that had served, or might serve again, as scholars' dwellings, as distinct from the more permanent halls. They
usually bore the name of their owner—like Peckwater Inn,
which gave its name to a Christ Church quadrangle on the
same site, or Tackley's Inn, which was a grammar hall in
1450. The property now known as the Golden Cross in
the Cornmarket was an inn in the old sense before it
became a hostelry in the new. It too belonged to Oseney;
and the carpenter may well have held his 'inn' on lease
from that abbey, or St. Frideswide's, or Godstow nunnery,
or even from St. John's Hospital outside the East gate—
where Magdalen College now stands. It is the cartularies and rent-rolls of these foundations that supply us
with the names and occupations of thousands of the
citizens.

The city of Oxford was laid out—historians cannot
agree why—in a grid pattern, presenting roughly rectangular blocks divided into long strips of various sizes, the
larger houses often lying behind or above a fringe of shops
(sometimes separate freeholds), and running lengthwise:
i.e. they were often L-shaped, end-on to the street and approached by an entry, as Kemp Hall—in the present High
Street—still is. The plans of such houses, as Dr. Pantin

[1] In Cambridge *hospicium* was translated 'hostel'; hence Garret Hostel.

has skilfully reconstructed them,[1] taken along with details provided by Chaucer, but not found in the analogues,
help us to visualize John's dwelling. On the ground floor
might be an open-roofed hall, perhaps with a parlour
or shop adjacent, over a cellar. Behind would be kitchen,
buttery, stables, privy. Many houses had a 'solar' (it
caught the sunlight) on the first floor, sometimes approached by external (stone) steps; but Chaucer mentions
only a 'bower', which gives on to the street—so the whole
of the street-frontage cannot be occupied by a hall. In
1403 New College leased the front shop of their hospice
(then called Gingevere Inn) in the Cornmarket to one
William Shrovesbury, a cordwainer, on condition that he
did not disturb folk in the solar above or in the cellar
below by excessive hammering (*pulsacio*); Dr. Pantin
infers that the front at least was merely timber-framed and
that the cellar was let separately (perhaps as an ale-house?).
Above the first floor, and under the roof, would be the
'cockloft'—perhaps partly floored to provide bedchambers
for Robin and Gill. A house designed for a teacher of
French in Catte Street in 1400 had a bedchamber in this
portion for the pupils he boarded. The upper floor, and
gable(s) would both have an overhang, or *gitee*. My own
hypothetical reconstruction[2] involves a double gable, one
over the hall, the other over 'bower' and 'chamber'. This
pattern certainly was not uncommon later;[3] but in the

[1] *Antiquaries Journal*, xxvii (1947), 120–50.

[2] Fig. 2*b*; Fig. 2*a* represents Dr. Pantin's view, and is perhaps preferable.

[3] For an early reference to a gable see OHS lxiv. 121. Houses with double gables
are shown in Agas's 16th-century plan (OHS xxxviii). Two such properties
survived in Queen St. till 1887 and in the High St. till about the same date: see
plates in OHS lxiv opp. pp. 180 and 210 (and cf. plate opp. p. 228) and photo-
graphs on pp. 26 and 42 in C. W. Judge, *Oxford Past and Present* (1971). An
interesting reference to a gable occurs in the *Register of Godstow Nunnery* (EETS
o.s. 129), i. 382. For a house with a little solar in the hall, and a great solar over
a cellar, see EETS o.s. 130, ii. 482; for an 'entryng' see ibid. 485.

A house corresponding roughly to plan (*b*) once stood at 126 High St. (Pantin,
op. cit., Fig. 8B). In the house designed for Wm. Kingsmill (see above) the

house that was formerly 46 The Broad the roof-tree ran parallel to the street, over a hall with an open roof. The fact that all John's household need ladders to get into the roof suggests that the improvised boats hang above the open roof of such a hall; and the bower must have a ceiling and a separate frontage: it clearly could not be visible from the roof where John hangs. The gable must have been quite long (and hence dark) since Nicholas insists that John is to lie far enough away from Alison not to be tempted by lustful thoughts—'no sinne, Nomoore in lookyng than ther shal in deede' (A 3590–1). Nicholas's hypocritical and sophistical gravity reaches its height when he thus turns both Old and New Testament to his purpose, and (it seems) alludes to the traditional teaching, reproduced in Mirk's *Festial*, that there was no copulation in the ark.[1]

He proposes that John should break through the gable when the flood rises and float out 'unto the gardin-ward, over the stable' (3572); and John duly includes (to his own undoing) an axe in his gear; so the gable-end must have been of light materials—presumably lath and plaster. Most Oxford tenements had a long, walled garden strip to the rear like those behind the houses in Holywell to this day; though the medieval garden walls were often of mud; and that many tenements also had stables, local deeds inform us.[2] John's would be empty, since his horse or horses were carrying Robin and Gill to London. The tubs hang from the baulks, i.e. beams of roughly squared

ground floor contained store-rooms, kitchen, stable, the first-floor chambers, latrine, etc. For a detailed description of an 'inn' that housed lodgers see OHS lxxxix. 45.

[1] EETS E.S. 96, p. 72. The assumed piety is adumbrated in l. 3216, which may bespeak clerkly familiarity with Masses *cum nota de beata virgine* such as were celebrated on most Saturdays at Balliol (OHS lxiv. 295); but see p. 31 above.

[2] e.g. OHS lxxxix. 167, *Godstow Reg.* ii. 415. The statutes of Queen's, on the other hand, enjoined that no horses were to be stabled within the college walls 'since the purity of the air affects the faculty for study'. At Oxford as at Cambridge college stables were often on the opposite side of the street.

timber, probably slightly curved, serving as tiebeams from
wall to wall; since they supported the kingposts, which
held the roof-tree, they would certainly be strong enough
to bear the troughs and their human contents (none are
heavy-weights). The happy trio are to wait in their tubs or
kimlins till the water rises to the eaves; by then it would
have covered all windows that might have been used as
exits, and, like the Deluge that they all have in mind,
drowned all their neighbours: which is why the presence
of these neighbours, when John eventually crashes down
to the 'celle' (3822)—the 'ground-sel' or ground floor—is
so piquant. If he drops right from the roof of the hall to
the floor, it is no wonder that he knocks himself out and
breaks his arm—and frightens Alison and Nicholas. By
the time this happens it is past lauds, so the neighbours
would be in any case astir, and would naturally rush in
from the street direct to the hall to see what the matter
was and 'to gauren on this man' (3827).

The other rooms, then, must lie alongside the hall.
Nicholas's is reached by a stair (presumably from the hall);
and the bower (the married pair's bedroom) where he and
Alison disport themselves, has a shot-window on to the
street, but it must be very low down for Absolon to be
able to knock on it, and for the kissing to take place:
'Unto his brest it raughte, it was so lowe' (3696); yet it is
high enough for him to have room to swing the coulter
(3810).[1] So the bower may have been over a low-ceilinged
shop; it would be empty at night, so that Absolon would
not be creating a disturbance, nor would his bleatings be
overheard. The 'shot-window' that Nicholas 'up dide'
(3801: 'threw open', not 'up') was evidently a small case-
ment:[2] probably square, about two feet by two feet, like

---

[1] The house illustrated in Judge, op. cit., p. 32, had windows on the first floor
low enough to be reached by a tall man.

[2] A shot-window was wide enough for a man to get through, according to
a Scots song: cf. *Oxford Book of Ballads*, ed. J. Kinsley (1969), p. 314.

later examples: no other instance of the term is found
before Gavin Douglas, who in the prologue to Book Seven
of his *Eneydos* gives a vignette of himself getting up in his
'chamber' on a winter morning, opening the shot-window
a little, and closing it with a shiver as he hears the hail-
stones 'hoppand on the thak and on the causay by'—
beating on the thatched roof (Oxford roofs too were
usually thatched) and on the causeway outside (Oxford
streets too were paved).[1]

Two-gabled houses at this date were perhaps 'presti-
gious': indeed this is the first vernacular application of the
Old French term 'gable' (the sense in *Piers Plowman*
A iii. 50 being different). If the house abutted directly
on to its neighbours (as most did), the entry into garden-
yard and stable would be incorporated in the ground-floor
plan. John naïvely says his charm (and doubtless makes
the sign of the cross) on the 'foure halves of the hous
aboute' (3481), but the emphasis in the next line—'and on
the thresshfold of the dore *withoute*'—suggests that it is
the inner walls that are in question, so it need not be free-
standing. The practice of making a cross on the threshold
persisted in rural districts among folk of John's kind, long
after the Reformation.

Nicholas's room is large ('all the chambre rong' when
he played his psaltery); and it has a stout door—John the
carpenter would see to that—fastened with a hasp (3470),
and with an inside latch; and either at the foot of the door,
or in a wall on the landing there is a dividing panel, or cat
hole. The cat was part of the medieval household, as
Chaucer indicates on another occasion (*CT* D 1775). Even
anchoresses (like those who lived where Merton's Mob
Quad now stands) were allowed to keep one; and the contemporary Pepys pattern book shows two drawn from life.
When Nicholas conveys provisions to his chamber he has

---

[1] In 1339 the Vice-Chancellor and the Mayor had been empowered to distrain
citizens to repair the *pavimentum* in front of the houses: OHS lxx. 137.

to do it surreptitiously ('ful softe', 3410)—presumably lest he should meet John on the stair. So normally he must have had full board—unless he took some meals in a tavern or baked-meat shop; but the whole action indicates that he was treated like a member of the household. John fusses about him as a modern landlady might.

Though some trades and occupations were confined to certain quarters of Oxford—vintners on the west side of St. Aldate's, fletchers to the south-east of Carfax, etc.— carpenters, not being shopkeepers, might be found in any parish. In 1290, for instance (and probably later), one Geoffrey a carpenter was living in a house in Kybald Street, near Merton, perhaps because he was working for that College, which owned it. John's house is not far from the forge of Gervase the smith, since Absolon has only to cross the street to reach it, and he can creep back to Alison's window before the heated coulter has time to cool. It was a pitch-black night (3731) and it would be at its darkest just before dawn. He would have to pick his way, as there might be firewood or even dung lying out- side some houses: in 1405 the abbot of Oscney was charged with littering the highway 'cum truncis juxta Elmehalle, ad grave damnum'.[1] Merely by being abroad at night Absolon laid himself open to suspicion: no honest man would leave his house after curfew (3645). At Cam- bridge the rules of the Guild of the Assumption stated that 'if any of the brethren be in the habit of wandering about the streets at night, or playing checkers or dice [in taverns?] or frequenting doubtful company' he risked expulsion.[2] Even in eighteenth-century Oxford every man *in statu pupillari* had to 'leave his can' when he heard the

---

[1] As late as 1514 dung from a garden was allowed to lie in the street until 'it amountith to the quantitie of a loade': OHS lxiv. 155; and 'blokks or other purprestours' [for which see OHS xviii. 205, 220] were allowed to lie for a week: Turner, *Selections from the Records of the City of Oxford*, p. 166.

[2] *Cambridge Gild Records*, ed. M. Bateson (*CAS* 8vo Ser. xxxix. 73, *sub anno* 1389).

mighty Tom strike its hundred and one at nine. Gervase
is hard at work on a plough or ploughs, preparing them
for use in the morning; which suggests that his forge is
not far from the outskirts of the town, and near a gate that
farmers would find convenient. But it must be within the
walls, since gates were shut at dusk. Smithgate, a small
gate closing a foot-passage near the north end of Catte
Street (it was small enough for rowdy students to throw it
into the Cherwell in 1264) neatly meets the requirement;
its name must derive from the presence of smiths in the
vicinity, near the arable land that stretched north of the
city. The street now called the Broad—just west of Smithgate—was formerly Horsemonger Street, where farriers
would be most in demand. Blacksmiths customarily
worked at night to early morning—the best time to repair gear, or 'tip' ploughshares that were needed on the
morrow—and they would make less disturbance in this
quarter than in the centre of the city. That they made
noise enough we know from some lively alliterative lines
written about this time:

> Swarte smekyd smethes smateryd with smoke
> Dryve me to deth with den of here dyntes.
> Sweche noyse on nyghtes ne herd men never . . .[1]

Besides making farming implements, they could—as Merton accounts testify—provide rings for a lenten veil, or
lugs for a college bell; and they were kept busy as farriers
when almost all travel was by horse. There was a guild of
Oxford blacksmiths in the fifteenth century. Why a smith
should swear by Saint Neot ('Note', 3771) remains as
mysterious to us as it was to the scribe who substituted

---

[1] K. Sisam, *Fourteenth-Century Verse and Prose* (1921), p. 169. In Gloucester,
and doubtless elsewhere, smiths carried on their trade in a street known as 'þe
smithys strete' (*Godstow Reg.* i. 146 (1289)). It must be noted, however, that
smiths were found in various parts of fourteenth-century Oxford, e.g. Henry
the Smith was living in Fish Street in 1377 (OHS lxiv. 123). A smith working at
his forge and shoeing a horse is shown in the contemporary MS. Bodl. 264, f. 107ʳ.

'seynt Eloi', patron saint of blacksmiths as well as of gold-smiths. Like the invocation of Saint Leonard in the *Hous of Fame*, it may be another sign of Chaucer's own East Anglian affiliations.

It is when we turn to look at Absolon and Alison that we see how ill the label of 'fabliau' befits this tale. The exactness in the description of their dress and accomplishments points back to the Prologue's portraits but also immerses us in the life of Oxford parishes and Oxford streets. Particularization begins with their names which, like all the other names in this tale and the Reeve's, can be found in Oxford, or Cambridge, documents; though the Biblical Absolon has its special appropriateness for this youth of luxuriant hair. But whereas Nicholas is the typical name for a clerk—Emden quotes a hundred examples—the name Absolon is not found except in city records. Only to a limited degree do he and Alison play traditional roles, as illustrated in the Provençal *Flamenca*, where courtship of the pretty young wife goes on at Mass. 'Kyrie, so kyrie, Jankyn syngyt merie, With aleyson' runs a fifteenth-century carol, using the name of the Wife of Bath's parish clerk, and punning on the name Alison and the *eleison* (mercy) of the *Kyrie*.[1] 'I preye you that you wol *rewe* [have mercy] on me' pleads our Absolon, acting the courtly lover (3362). The aforementioned carol offers a succinct catalogue of his duties as parish clerk. He leads in the intoning of the *Kyrie*, reads the Epistle, sings the Sanctus, and carries round the paxbrede—the form in which, after the mid thirteenth century, the kiss of peace, given by the priest before receiving the Host, was trans-

---

[1] R. L. Greene, *A Selection of English Carols* (1962), no. 98. Cf. no. 96, and:

> Hwenne heo to chirche cometh
>   To the haliday
> Heo biholdeth Wadekin
>   Mid swithe gled eye.
> Atom his hire paternoster
>   Biloken in hire teye [case].   (EETS o.s. 49, p. 190)

mitted to the congregation: the priest kissed a framed image of (usually) the Crucifixion, with a handle behind, enabling the clerk to bear it to each member of the congregation, duly wiping it with a napkin: an ideal opportunity for an infatuated clerk to hint his desires and cast a loving look.[1] So Absolon swings his censer, at the offertory, ardently towards the women of the congregation—perhaps sitting separately, as they still do in some places in Europe. He adds to his impiety by declining to accept the goodwives' oblations: these might be in either coin, or bread and wine—perhaps still at this date brought up to the altar rail with hands muffled in a linen cloth; up to the Reformation wives brought the holy bread (*pain bénit*) that was cut up (by the parish clerk) and distributed by the priest from a 'hamper', 'according to every man's degree'. By 1450 and perhaps earlier the regular offering was a penny on Sunday (the 'dominical penny') and on each of the great festivals (Chaucer's 'halidays', 3309, 3340).[2] These and similar offerings at churchings, weddings, and burials produced half the income of an Oxford city incumbent except in the rich churches of St. Mary's (endowed, as Cardinal Newman's career reminds us, with the tithes of Littlemore) and St. Peter's in the East, which enjoyed the tithes of Wolvercote and the manor of Holywell, and which Henry III had bestowed on Merton—connections only lately broken. Of the other eighteen or so churches not all were parochial; one, St. Edward's near Blue Boar Lane, was probably suppressed about the time of our tale:

[1] Several fine paxes are to be seen in the Royal Ontario Museum, Toronto (L.960.9.21 etc.).

[2] Cf. OHS xcvii. 125 top. For the survival of the practice see Fitzherbert's *Husbandry* (1534), f. 9b. A clerk's duties sometimes included the carrying of holy water to every house in the parish on Sundays: see J. W. Legg, Pref. to *The Clerk's Book of 1549* (Henry Bradshaw Society, 1903). In the fifteenth century Oseney provided wheat for making the *panis benedictus* for the parish church at Cudlington (Oxon.) and appointed the holy-water clerk: OHS xcvii. 125. For duties and payments of the parish clerk at St. Mary's (including reading the Epistle) see OHS lxxiii. 286–7.

an aftermath of the Plague.[1] Fraternities (the 'friendly' or 'burial' societies of a later age) were dying out for the same reason.

But Chaucer speaks only of the wives of the parish as at church and speaks of them thrice (3309, 3341, 3350). Did they go to church on some holy-days without their husbands? I think they did, for this reason: in the obit book of Queen's College, some feasts are marked to be kept by all (*omnino*) but others as 'ferianda ab operibus mulierum'; women are to abstain from ordinary occupations on these days—mostly, but not entirely, the feasts of female saints (Margaret, Agatha, Lucy, etc.). The only other Kalendar so marked is in a Hereford missal of *c.* 1350, but there is some evidence for the practice in the Worcester diocese, and possibly at Cambridge.[2] Absolon then, on such a 'haliday', would have no competition; and Alison looked her brightest on such occasions, when she 'leet hir werk' (3311), and all women put on their finery (cf. *Piers Plowman* B v. 110).

All a clerk's ecclesiastical functions contributed to make an Absolon a familiar figure in his parish; and he could show off and make eyes at his mistress without rousing suspicion in a university rival, for the scholars would in general attend services in St. Mary's or a college chapel, or possibly a friary church. John, like the speaker in the Jankin carol, would have no difficulty in recognizing Absolon 'by his mery note' as he sang his love-song to the moon and Alison (3365–6); and when the clerk quavers 'brokkinge as a nightingale' (3377) he is doing exactly what Jankin did in that carol—'cracking notes an hundred on a knot' [i.e. at a time]—and doing exactly what had

---

[1] The transepts of Merton Chapel provided the parish church for St. John's parish. Conversely, at Cambridge Gonville used St. Michael's parish church near by. Thus Town and Gown came together more than they do now.

[2] OHS lvi, p. xxviii. The phrase 'Cristes owne werkes for to wirche' certainly refers to a Mass: cf. 'Godes werkes for to worche', *Layfolks' Mass Book* (EETS o.s. 71), p. 133, l. 168. For offerings on such occasions see ibid., p. 232.

stirred Wiclif's spleen at Oxford and elsewhere—the 'veyn japis' of 'deschaunt, countre note and organ and smale brekynge, þat stirriþ veyn men to daunsynge more than to mornynge'.[1]

Absolon is in the situation described in the fabliaux and *exempla* that had already been given English guise in *Dame Sirith* and the interlude *De Clerico et Puella*. He is wooing a woman whose husband is from time to time conveniently absent (in *Dame Sirith* he has gone to Boston in Lincolnshire); and, like those wooers, he resorts to 'menes and brocages' (3375), go-betweens or panders (male or female), to urge his suit. In *Dame Sirith* the dame plays this role; in the Interlude the clerk who 'hauntes scole' (i.e. attends lectures) and is in love with Maid Malkin, appeals to Mome Eluys to help him. Absolon also tries other ploys, including presents of wafers 'piping hot', as today he might send a bumper box of candy—but with this difference, that the wafers (delicacies that might be compounded of cheese, eggs, milk, sugar, ginger, and the belly of a pike) would be purveyed, and conveyed, by waferwomen, regularly employed in such amatory intrigues: Chaucer associates them with bawds in his Pardoner's Tale (C 479); Beaumont and Fletcher's plays (cit. O.E.D.) provide illustrations of their dealings.

Being parish clerk was only a part-time occupation. Absolon would get certain customary fees, and, strictly, every household was required to give the clerk a loaf at Christmas, eggs at Easter, sheaves at harvest: conceivably the 'offerings' that Absolon refuses (3350) included such items. A century or so later a holy-water clerk at Cambridge who was a draper by trade earned from twenty to forty

---

[1] See K. Sisam, op. cit., p. 123. Absolon sings 'somtime a loud quinible' (3332)—an octave above the treble: the term is found elsewhere only in Skelton, who was well read in Chaucer: 'They finger their fiddles and cry in quinibles' (*Works*, ed. Dyce, ii. 434). For song accompanied by gittern (3333) cf. *P.Pl.* B xiii 233. The only surviving example of a gittern like Absolon's is illustrated in the Report of the National Art Collections Fund for 1963.

shillings for his services.[1] But the Wife of Bath's Jankin, holding the same office, was decidedly poor. There was nothing, however, to prevent him marrying, and we know of at least one parish clerk who did. Meanwhile Absolon laboured in his vocation as barber-surgeon. In that capacity he may have belonged to the guild of university barbers, of which the regulations, dating from 1348, survive. Its members were formally enrolled as *privilegiati*, i.e. members of a craft employed in the university and owing allegiance to the Chancellor (whose jurisdiction extended as far as Botley and the third arch of Folly Bridge), and subject to his courts, not the Mayor. A shave was an expensive luxury and few university men shaved more than once a week: it cost a halfpenny to be shaved in one's room (twenty pence in modern money, or more). No man might be shaved on Sunday unless he had to deliver a sermon. In Queen's the barber had to wash the scholars' heads: washerwomen were expressly forbidden to do so. The barber was often, like Absolon, a bloodletter, and regular bloodletting (another monastic custom) was widely practised. But strictly speaking a church official like Absolon ought not to have drawn blood. *Ecclesia abhorret a sanguine!*

Nicholas has Absolon's tonsorial skill in mind when he quips 'a beard, a beard!' after the misdirected kiss (3742) —a locution echoed in the Reeve's Tale: 'Yet kan a millere make a clerkes berd' (4096). But it is far from being his only skill. He is a man of parts. Such a youth could have acquired some education at one of the several grammar halls that in fourteenth-century Oxford were attached, or adjacent to, certain colleges (having been intended primarily for boys of founders' kin): the best-known being the school of John Cornwall and Richard Pencrich in Merton Street, mentioned by Trevisa as having inaugu-

---

[1] *Cambridge Borough Documents*, p. 120. The same document (see ibid., p. 103), shows a holy-water clerk living in Trinity Hostel as exempt from Poll Tax; he was perhaps a member of the university.

rated the method of teaching Latin in the English tongue that led to the abandonment of French as the medium of instruction in Chaucer's time. Equipped with the rudiments of Latin grammar, Absolon could have learnt to 'make a chartre of lond or acquitaunce' (3327) from some manual of conveyancing. One such formulary is associated with late fourteenth-century Oxford, and copies of it survive. It begins with a model for a *carta feodis simplicis* (the Man of Law's 'fee simple', A 319) and ends with 'acquietancia facta per ordinarium alicui administratori bonorum alicuius ab intestato decendentis'—a model of an 'acquitance' made to someone administering the goods of a man dying intestate.[1] The Oxford monastic cartularies abound in just such documents; and one Merton charter actually has an Absolon granting land to Walter the smith:[2] a hint of the kind of acquaintanceship posited in our tale. One of the two Oxford scriveners who used the formulary quoted above was teaching letter-writing and conveyancing before 1390—running, in fact, a business school, for which parish clerks would be likely pupils in a town like Oxford, which was essentially a collection of tradesmen. To judge from the length and number of extant deeds, Absolon might earn substantial fees for engrossing, and perhaps too for procuring witnesses: whether they were fellow tradesmen, or neighbours of the parties concerned, as parish clerk he would know them all. And since many of the town deeds had to do with Oseney, he would be well known to officials of that abbey, so can plausibly inquire, as if on business, about the missing carpenter (3661). He might in time rise to the status of town clerk or coroner's

---

[1] See H. G. Richardson, 'Business training in Medieval Oxford', *American Historical Review*, xlvi (1941), 259–80, and *BRUO*, s.v. Thomas Sampson.

[2] Stephenson's transcripts of Merton Archives, V.2488 (unpublished). Absolon a parish (?) clerk and Gervase a carpenter figure in the same Oxford document: OHS lxxxix. 214–15. For earlier Absolons see ibid., p. 205, xc. 554 (*filius Roberti presbiteri*), and *Godstow Reg.* i. 215. For a John Carpenter see OHS lxxiii. 110, and for another Gervase ibid. 20.

clerk; though even the former post was not necessarily full-time: John Langrisshe, Oxford's town clerk from 1344 to 1350, was also a brewer. But certainly a spry parish clerk could make enough, if a bachelor, to spend on fine clothes and shoes and presents for a mistress.

Varied as Absolon's avocations were, he still had time to join in the dances held in the streets or the fields outside the town—the sport and play at Oseney would probably include dancing. It is just here, where our local knowledge is most defective, that Chaucer's is most precise:

> In twenty manere koude he trippe and daunce
> After the scole of Oxenforde tho (A 3328–9)

—where 'school' must mean 'style' or 'fashion', as in 'after the scole of Stratforde atte Bowe'; in the present context it is in townish counterpoint to the academic schools of Absolon's rival; and the context likewise suggests that the style was florid, that he danced with bravura. But whether solo, or in a pair, or a team, remains uncertain. We should perhaps think of dancing in the Morris style and in the ornate costume that solo Morris dancers still sometimes affect. Such dancing has a long tradition in the Oxford area and the neighbouring villages of Berkshire, where the teams still preserve distinctive local styles and routines. Tailors danced in the Oxford streets on the Eve of St. John's Day in 1306, but to what pattern we know not.

Equally precise, and equally unverifiable, is Chaucer's allusion to Oxford miracle-plays:

> Somtyme, to shewe his lightnesse and maistrye,
> [Absolon] pleyeth Herodes upon a scaffold hye
> (3383–4)

—though there is unimpeachable evidence that the part of Herod appealed to the ham actor who could tear a passion to tatters, not only on the pageant wagon, but 'in the strete also', that is even when off-stage. Hence the description of the angry Duke of Suffolk in the Paston Letters: 'ther was

never no man that playd Herrod in Corpus Crysty play
better and more agreable to hys pageaunt than he did.'
'*Irabit*', says the Chester stage-direction: 'he must rage';
and at Chester he was gorgeously crowned in gold foil.[1]
The play would offer another occasion for Absolon to
impress his Alison: for like her namesake the Wife of Bath
(they both wear the married woman's 'couvrechef' or
'voluper'), she would not be one to keep away from 'pleyes
of miracles' (D 557), any more than from 'processiouns'
(D 556). About Oxford processions we have some evidence, which indicates that they ended up as picnics.[2] To
say that there is no such evidence for Oxford miracle cycles
is simply to say that its Guild records are few and Council
records fragmentary. But if the small town of Thame
twelve miles away had a play of Herod and the Three
Kings, and if Cambridge (by 1350) had a guild play called
Ludus Filiorum Israel (probably the Deliverance from
Egypt, as at Newcastle) it is probable that Oxford had
similar performances, organized either by a parish guild
(as at Cambridge) or by craft guilds (as was more usual).[3]

At Oxford there were guilds of butchers, cooks, shoemakers, mercers, merchants, glovers, skinners, smiths,
tailors, weavers—enough to stage a complete cycle. (Is
Peter Quince's company of weaver, tinker, tailor, joiner,
bellow-mender, a vestigial epitome of such an assembly?)
Elsewhere the play of Herod was acted by the mercers
(Beverly), the goldsmiths (York), or the smiths (*Ludus
Coventriae*); but those very variations indicate that it
might equally well be allocated to the barbers, the blood-
letters who could massacre the Innocents. Thus either
shipmen or carpenters took the Noah play; and it is to the

---

[1] *Chester Plays* (EETS E.S. 72), p. 201; *Paston Letters*, ed. N. Davis (1958),
p. 87. It is ironical that a once-popular Midland locution, 'to play Hamlet', had
exactly the same connotation.
[2] *A Fifteenth Century School Book*, ed. W. A. Nelson (1956), p. 26.
[3] See *CAS* 8vo Ser. xxxix. 51 ff., and R. M. Wilson, *The Last Literature of
Medieval England* (1969), p. 212. (See also p. 126 below.)

apocryphal episode found in the York version of this play that Nicholas appeals when persuading the carpenter to follow his counsel of secrecy:

> 'Hastow nat herd,' quod Nicholas, 'also
> The sorwe of Noe with his felaweshipe,
> Er that he myghte gete his wyf to shipe?
> Him hadde be lever, I dar wel undertake,
> At thilke tyme, than alle hise wetheres blake,
> That she hadde had a ship hir-self allone . . .'
>   (A 3538–43)[1]

In England this story is peculiar to the mystery plays— with the possible exception of a scene in the Cædmon manuscript, plausibly associated with it by Gollancz. Nicholas assumes that John will have heard Noah uttering on the 'scaffaud' such a lament as the Towneley play gives him:

> Yee men that has wifis: whyls they ar yong
> If ye luf youre lifis, chastice thare tong:
> Me thynk my hert ryfis, both levyr and long,
> To se sich stryfis, wedmen emong;
> But I, as have I blys,
> Shall chastyse this . . .
> I shall make the still as stone, begynnar of blunder,
> I shall bete the bak and bon, and breke all in sonder

—the scene, I suggest, that is depicted on the margin of the Bodleian manuscript of the Alexander romance, but described by M. R. James simply as a puppet-show.[2] It is played there, as here, on a 'scaffold'; and the poet who as Clerk of Works was responsible for erecting lists and scaffolds for jousts at Smithfield, and who describes in detail Theseus' 'theatre' (A 1885), placing Theseus'

---

[1] See Anna J. Mill, *PMLA* lvi (1941), 613 ff.; and *The Cædmon Manuscript*, ed. I. Gollancz (1927), p. xlv. Nicholas's insistence on secrecy recalls the ancient legend, cited by Miss Mill, that God enjoined secrecy on Noah.

[2] Preface to his edition of the MS. (1933), p. 18, and J. J. Jusserand in *An English Miscellany Presented to F. J. Furnivall* (1901), p. 192 (with plate). For the scene in the Towneley cycle see EETS E.S. lxxi. 35.

herald on a scaffold (A 2533), specifies that Absolon plays on a 'scaffold hye'—i.e. on a two-storey pageant-wagon. Royalty seems generally to have been presented on the upper storey of such a wagon: the *Ludus Coventriae* stage-direction reads: 'Herowdys scaffold xall unclose, shewing Herowdis in astat' i.e. seated on a throne above the crowd.

Absolon the actor, clad in Herod's 'gleterynge golde' robes and kingly crown, was Absolon the dandy, who as a barber could curl his own hair, and could spend the money he earned by his acting on his own adornment—symbolized by those natty shoes of his, with the front cut out in a design representing the East rose window of St. Paul's, which must have cost him a good deal more than sixpence a pair, the average price for shoes. He would have bought them in the cordwainery, which occupied the area in the Cornmarket where Woolworth's now stands. It was during the excavations here that many medieval shoes came to light—usually with a single black-tanned cowhide sole, flesh-side up, sewn to the upper, which was hair-side up, and shaved down to 2/3 mm. on the flesh side. Many of the shoes found, even elegant women's pumps such as Alison would wear, had been soled and heeled.[1] But Oxford cordwainers made a good living and theirs was one of the most flourishing of the Oxford guilds. Indeed in 1321 the admission fee was so high that the Chancellor complained that shoes were becoming too dear 'to the great injury of scholars and others'.[2]

The rest of Absolon's pocket-money he spent on 'brew-house and taverne' (3334); they were numerous enough. Town and gown mingled (or quarrelled) in them: hence

[1] *Oxoniensia*, xxiii. 75. In 1380 there were at least eighteen cordwainers in Oxford (one 'atte hurne' presumably had a corner shop), three smiths, and sixteen carpenters: OHS xviii. 25, etc. According to the 14th-century assizes shoemakers lived in the Northgate hundred—i.e. the Cornmarket: OHS lxxiii, p. xviii.

Shoes with designs resembling a rose-window were illustrated in the exhibition 'Chaucer's London' (1972).

[2] OHS lxx. 346; see ibid., p. 97, for the cordwainers' 'mystery' (*mesterium*).

the participation of the university in the assise of bread and ale, and the clause in Henry III's grant of privileges to the effect that wines were to be sold 'communiter et indifferenter tam clericis quam laicis' from the same barrel.

It is time to leave the town and go with Absolon to Oseney. He would reach the abbey by paths north or south of the castle, leading to Quaking Bridge and Bookbinders' Bridge, or he could cross the river by Hythe Bridge, built about 1190 (as Salter thought) to enable the parishioners across the river to attend the new church of Saint Thomas, then recently canonized. The main stream of the Thames (down which Matilda had escaped from the castle in 1142) in those days ran under this bridge, and worked the Castle mills; the Oseney stream, now the main one, which John might have crossed had he gone to the grange, was still fordable, but the bridge across it was rebuilt by the Abbot of Oseney before 1373. The flow was controlled by a lock higher up, owned by Rewley Abbey (supplying a head of water for another mill) and in dry weather the Oseney stream was a mere trickle.

Both castle and abbey were places of public resort. A century later an Oxford schoolbook gives us a glimpse of 'all the yonge folkes almost of this towne' running 'to the castell to se a bere batyde with fers dogges within the wallys'. There would be undergraduates among any such crowd, for they were accustomed to stay up during vacations; and the source just cited states that 'ther is more discontenuance in Oxforde then in eny other universite. For it hath been nowe a moneth togedre that no scole hath be kept, and after the comyn worde they call this tyme vacacioun, and that not amysse, for many men that tyme levyth all studyes and gevyth them all togedre to sportes and plays.'[1]

---

[1] Nelson (ed. cit. p. 49 n. 2 above), pp. 26 and 27. A Bear Yard figures in an early map of Cambridge, and a 'bearward' in *Oxford Records* (ed. Turner), p. 284,

But it was in the fields just outside the city and abbey walls that town and gown mostly took their recreation. To the north, Beaumont fields were a favourite playground of the scholars.[1] And to the east lay the 'Campus pitts', where in the seventeenth century, if not earlier, the Wits would take their walks. The name refers to the pits of marl or clay at the east end of Milham ford, now the site of St. Hilda's College; and the Campus could be reached by a footbridge higher up the Cherwell—from which the Monk of Farne fell on a certain occasion.[2] I suggest that when Chaucer adapts the ancient tale from the *Theaetetus* of Thales, the absent-minded philosopher who 'walked in the feeldes for to prye / Upon the sterres' (3458–9) and substitutes 'marl-pit' for the well into which the Greek philosopher fell, he has Campus Pits in mind. Curiously enough there was a well in this area too, named after Saint Edmund of Abingdon, patron of St. Edmund Hall; the well was so called, says Anthony Wood, because the Saint did there 'often according to his manner convers in privat with God'. It too now lies within the bounds of St. Hilda's. Socrates ascribes the story to a clever Thracian maid who says that Thales was so eager to know what was going on in the heavens that he could not see what was before his feet. But this jest, says Socrates, is equally applicable to all philosophers: for the philosopher is wholly unacquainted with his next-door neighbour—the very charge that the Eagle brings against Chaucer in the *Hous of Fame*, where as elsewhere he presents himself as bemused:

> But of thy verray neighebores,
> That duellen almost at thy dores,
> Thou herist neyther that ne this.
>
> (649–51)

---

[1] Cf. *Early Middle English Verse and Prose*, ed. Bennett and Smithers (1966), p. 163, l. 136, and the passage cit. H. B. Workman, *John Wyclif* (1926), i. 52.

[2] See *The Meditations of the Monk of Farne*, ed. D. Farmer (Studia Anselmiana, xli, 1957), pp. 141 ff.

A contemporary reader would quickly take the point of the marl-pit: marl was used for many purposes—including the fertilizing and the 'ramming' or 'backing' of banks and millponds: Cambridge (and doubtless other towns) had similar clay-pits on its outskirts: the Perse School at Cambridge was built in 1574 on the site of 'the Old Clay Pits'.[1] Marl was still being dug in some places for such uses in the nineteenth century.

But Absolon, a townsman, goes with his friends to Oseney, 'him to disporte and playe' (3660). Here Oseney probably means Oseney Mead or Bulstake Mead—a name that itself suggests the sport of bull-baiting. Indeed, the name provides perhaps the earliest example of 'stake' meaning a post to which an animal is fastened. The mead was held by the abbey, and not cultivated in strips, but open for free grazing.[2] At Oseney Absolon could easily slip into the abbey precincts; the laity were allowed free access to the nave, and Absolon's clerical status might admit him elsewhere.[3] Presumably as the monks are leaving choir after service, he meets a 'cloisterer': the term, taken with Chaucer's other use of it (A 259), suggests an ordinary monk, perhaps a novice (though the knowledgeable scribe of one manuscript specifies that he is a 'chanoune cloisterer'), who could chat with him in the cloister. The monk says enough about John to indicate that he knew his usual movements and that John was in the regular employ of the abbey. Oseney abbey was a small town in itself, more than one trade being carried on in its precincts—including a tannery and a book-bindery (Austin

---

[1] *Cambridge Borough Records*, p. 145. A tithe award cit. M. Gelling, *Place-Names of Oxfordshire* (1953), i. 24 but not at present accessible evidently refers to marl grounds in the immediate vicinity of Oxford: cf. Clay Close on the map cited ibid., p. 131, and Chalkpit Field, p. 61.

[2] For the meadows and bridges near Oseney see OHS xc, *ad fin.*

[3] In the 1340s students were accused of disturbing divine service in the Abbey on feasts of the Church: OHS N.S. iv. 174. They also caused trouble at Godstow: ibid., p. 173.

canons were given to book-making; a passage on the
site was still known fifty years ago as Bookbinders Yard);
and it employed its own teamsters, and ploughmen, and
owned a mill, and weirs (to provide its fish for fast days)
on the river. There would always be jobs for a carpenter,
including the building or repair of houses on the abbey's
city properties; and there would always be need of timber,
if only for firewood.[1] John, if he had not been cooped up
in his kimlin, might have been off on his 'stot', or with
horse and cart, to inspect newly felled timber or look over
beams stored for seasoning at the grange. Absolon assumes, and so must we, that it was some distance off—
further than Wytham but probably no further than Wych-
wood, the largest timbered area easily accessible from
Oseney—and that John would have had to stay the night.
Another John, surnamed Branch, when employed as
master-carpenter at All Souls, spent two days in Cumnor
Wood choosing oaks given for the purpose by the Abbot
of Abingdon.[2] Most abbeys had granges, sometimes used
by the abbot as an occasional residence, like one surviving
at Longworth near Oxford.[3]

[1] *Oxoniensia*, xvii. 124, cf. 138. The Abbey hired a carpenter for an entire
year in 1474: OHS ci. 305. For interesting details of repairs done in the Abbey
see ibid., pp. 212–13.

[2] See *Accounts of the Obedientiary of Abingdon* (Camden Soc. N.S. li, 1892),
p. 124, and *Berks. Arch. Soc. Journal*, iv (1948–9), 84.

Few Oseney account rolls survive. The Cartulary shows how the scattered
properties were grouped into bailiwicks in the 13th century. A canon was
resident bailiff in six of the bailiwicks, sending their produce to the Abbey:
OHS ci. 184.

[3] Landlords usually provided timber for the repair of copyholds: cf. A. Clark,
Godstow Register (EETS O.S. 129), i. 85. Oseney had woods at Kidlington, eight
miles away (*Oseney Register*, EETS O.S. 133, i. 98) and properties at Weston,
The Bartons, Hook Norton, Bourton, Watlington, and a few other places; but
none of them are in heavily wooded areas. For a description and drawings of
a monastic grange at Charney Bassett, Berks., see Turner, *Domestic Architecture*,
pp. 153–5. (See also p. 126 below.) For Oseney granges see *Register* ii. xxiv.

When the abbey leased the rectory of Stone (Bucks.) in 1474 it appears that
it was understood that repairs would be undertaken by carpenters (etc.) supplied
by the abbey: OHS xcviii. 171.

Oseney, with its extensive city properties, its tithes, and parish dues, and riparian rights all making for intimate connections with the citizens, belongs to the town-interest in our tale. And its demolition at the Reformation—when its stones and six of its seven fine bells were carted off to the King's new college of Christ Church—was in one sense a triumph of gown over town. Our tale has a similar outcome. Absolon's love-making is a transparent parody of a clerk's 'courtoisie': for it is always clerks, not the bourgeoisie, who are credited with speaking 'schille', skilfully, in love. We know what to expect when Absolon complains of an itching mouth, claims to mourn 'like a lamb after the teat', and carefully wipes his lips before kissing. True, Nicholas overreaches himself in more than one sense; but he has the last laugh. The tables, or the tubs, are turned. 'Blessed be alwey a lewed man / That noght but oonly his bileve kan': so John had moralized over the clerk who fell into the marl, and over Nicholas when he thinks him crazed by study. But he himself falls into the trap a clerk prepares for him. And at the end it is John who is 'holde wood in al the toun; / For every clerk anonright heeld with oother' (3846–7). Thus the gown, the university-interest, asserts itself; and in Nicholas we have a foretaste of 'that playful and caressing suavity of manner' which Max Beerbohm (himself its last embodiment) was to detect as the dangerous concomitant of the Oxford mind.

Yet at the end '*every* wight gan laughen of this stryf'. 'When Oxford draws knife, all England's soon at strife' ran the old adage. For once, however, the strife is subsumed in laughter. No matter if it be the broad laughter of fabliau, it puts town and gown on happier terms than they often were. The sense of holiday established by Nicholas's melodies, Alison's springtime beauty, Absolon's snow-white surplice and merry dance overspreads the elements of coarseness and cuckolding that provided

the original motif of the tale; and despite himself the sour
and melancholic Reeve, who professes that 'me list not
play for age', is to prove susceptible to it. A rigorist critic
may object to that kind of inference. But it is part of the
unique achievement of the tales that they keep constantly
within the range of our remembrance the varied responses
of a listening cavalcade.

III

THE MEN OF MERTON[1]

Two men named by Chaucer—and not at random—had close associations with the university of Oxford. To 'philosophical' Strode he dedicates his greatest poem, while his Nun's clerkly priest cites Bishop Bradwardine in the same breath as Boethius and Augustine; giving us reason to think, in view of the preceding references to 'altercacioun' and *disputationes* 'in scole' (*CT* B 4427), that 'this swete preest, this goodly man, sir John', may be himself an Oxford graduate. Both Bradwardine and Strode were Mertonians; and the respect Chaucer accords them is a mark both of the pre-eminence of Oxford and within Oxford of the college that had provided six of the university's Chancellors within a century.

About the early material and intellectual history of Merton we know, fortunately, more than is yet known, or may ever be known, of any similar institution. Its intellectual development can be traced partly in the careers of its *alumni*, partly in the records of its library. The latter (exemplarily edited by Powicke) are remarkable for their

---

[1] The biographical and bibliographical information in this chapter is largely derived from A. B. Emden, *A Biographical Register of the University of Oxford to A.D. 1500* (three vols., 1957–9; the Additions in vol. iii should be noted), and F. M. Powicke, *The Medieval Books of Merton College* (1931). Recent studies of Wiclif by K. B. McFarlane (1952), J. A. Robson (1961), and G. Leff (1968) are also pertinent. A valuable account of the relation of Bradwardine to Bacon is included in 'The Pseudo-Aristotelian *Sirr Al-Asrar* and Three Oxford Thinkers' by M. Manzalaoui, in *Arabic and Islamic Studies in Honor of H. A. R. Gibb*, ed. G. Makdisi (1965). J. A. Weisheipl's study of 'Curriculum of the Faculty of Arts at Oxford in the early Fourteenth Century' (*Medieval Studies*, xxvi (1964), 142–85) is indispensable preliminary reading.

fullness, the former for their variety. Take John Mauduit as an example: fellow in 1309, first bursar in 1310–11, he returned to Oxford for further study in 1319; encouraged by the famous bibliophile-bishop Richard of Bury, he was one of the first Mertonians to display astronomical interests: he composed an astronomical table, and 'bilious' Bale credited him with a geometrical tractate *De Corda Recta et Umbra*; but Merton knew him also as a physician, and a theologian; his tractatus *De Doctrina Theologica* survives. The said Richard of Bury also had to do, in his career at court, with another great Merton master, Walter Burley, 'doctor planus et perspicuus', Aristotelian commentator, opponent of Ockham, and author of a work on logic that is used by modern practitioners of formal logic, besides a popular hand-book of classical lore, *De Vita et Moribus Philosophorum*. When Chaucer has the wife of Bath appeal to the Almagest he may be citing Burley.[1] We cannot follow Bale and Leland in assigning to Merton Richard of Wallingford, famed for his invention of astronomical instruments including the Albion ('All by one') or great clock that told the movements of sun, moon, and planets as well as the times and seasons.[2] But Wallingford's astronomical studies during the second period of his residence in Oxford (c. 1318–27) may well have attracted the attention of Simon Bredon, who was a fellow of Merton from 1330 (or earlier) to 1341, doctor of medicine in 1355, and from 1366 till his death prebendary of Wightring in

---

[1] See R. Steele, *Chaucer and the Almagest* (1920), and p. 80 below. Burley's *In Physicam Aristotelis Expositio et Quaestiones* was printed at Venice in 1501 (repr. 1968). For his other works see C. Martin's study in OHS N.S. xvi. 194. For his Commentary on the *Politics* see L. S. Daly in *Essays in Medieval History Presented to Bertie Wilkinson* (1969), pp. 270–81.

[2] The spurious lines in the Paris MS. of the Miller's Tale (see p. 73 below) give Nicholas an albion as well as an astrolabe.

For Wallingford's treatises (shortly to be published by J. D. North) see *Fasciculus J. W. Clark dicatus* (1899) pp. 56–61, J. D. Price, *The Equatorie of the Planetis* (1955), pp. 127–8, and J. D. North, *Review of English Studies*, N.S. xx (1969), 259 n. 1.

Chichester, where he lived under the shadow of a great benefactor of the college, Bishop Reed. Bredon too was an astronomer and physician, who compiled some dozen tables, including one entitled *Nomina Instrumentorum Astrolabii*; he left Merton these and other such volumes, including a text of Ptolemy's *Quadripartitus* (probably the chief source of Chaucer's astronomy), and the works of Chaucer's 'Arnold of the Newe Toun' (*CT* G 1428), along with his 'larger astrolabe'; so it is not surprising that the *Equatory of the Planets* (in which Dr. Price some years ago found Chaucer's name) used plausibly to be ascribed to Bredon.[1] But like his predecessors he was more than a scientist: he wrote on the *Ethics* of Aristotle, and his copy of the *Sentences* is now in Oriel. Following him came Richard Swyneshead, who quite literally made his name as a mathematician, for he was dubbed *calculator*, after his *Liber Calculationum*;[2] and the Merton scholars who were concerned with the mathematics of motion, and 'the intension and remission of forms' are beginning to be known as the Oxford Calculators.

Amongst the natural philosophers it was another Mertonian, John Dumbleton, whose reputation stood highest.[3] He became a fellow before Bredon left the college and was still there in 1348, at work on his great *Summa Logicae et Philosophiae Naturalis*; and William of Heytesbury, who wrote *Termini Naturales* and *Regulae Solvendi Sophismata*, and became Chancellor of the University by 1370, was his exact contemporary. Dr. Weisheipl very properly linked

[1] He left his copy of Profacius' Almanac (a work referred to in the *Equatory*) to his friend Richard Campsall (*not* the fellow of Merton of that name).

[2] It would distinguish him from various other Swinesheads at Oxford and Cambridge: see J. A. Weisheipl in OHS N.S. xvi. 231, and *Medieval Studies*, xxxi (1969). As a common noun the word is known only from the Reeve's Tale (A 4262, to which Keats's use alludes). Miss Janet Colman analyses Roger Swineshead's *De Motibus Naturalibus* (which is related to a treatise of Bradwardine's) in a forthcoming paper on Jean de Ripa.

[3] See Weisheipl, 'The Place of John Dumbleton in the Merton School', *Isis*, 1 (1959), 439.

them together in his important studies of early fourteenth-century physics and the Merton 'School'.

The interest in 'natural science' displayed by these scholars was a direct extension of the pattern of studies obtaining in fourteenth-century Oxford. The Arts student began at the Trivium, with its emphasis on logic ('old' and 'new'). To logic also Merton made notable contributions, notably in the work of Richard Campsall, whose monument can still be seen in the college chapel, and whose works are now being edited for the Pontifical Institute by Dr. Synan: Campsall's *Quaestiones* on Aristotle's *Prior Analytics* provide a convenient sample of the topics argued in the Oxford Schools, and glanced at by the Nun's Priest (B 4427 f.)—as well as instances of 'insolubilia' of the kind that fascinated Bertrand Russell. It is this sort of fine-spun syllogistic argument that the Miller of the Reeve's Tale seems to be sneering at when he says to the Cambridge clerks:

> 'Myn hous is streit, but ye han lerned art;
> Ye konne by *argumentes* make a place
> A myle brood, of twenty foot of space . . .' (A 4122–4)

The work of Campsall shows that a logician also thought of himself as a philosopher; and to the Clerk of the Prologue 'Aristotle and his philosophy' need not have meant more than the *Prior Analytics*: Langland associates Aristotle with logic rather than science. But, demure as that clerk is, he presents himself as a travelled man who had learnt his tale from Petrarch, that 'worthy clerk', at Padua; hardly the journey an undergraduate would make, but not unlikely for an older man: Italian friars like Pizzegoti were not the only scholars to go between Padua and Oxford.[1]

---

[1] Oxford clerks studied at both Padua and Bologna; Bolognese merchants came regularly to London, where Chaucer probably had dealings with them. Chaucer's rendering of Petrarch's tale may have some connection with the letter from Philip de Mézières to Richard II in 1395 urging the king to read 'le cronique autentique . . . de Grisildis, escripte par le solemnel docteur et souverain poete, Maistre Francois Petrac' (BM MS. Royal 20 B vi, f. 49). If Richard took this advice he probably read the story in its French version, as Chaucer did.

Since the Clerk 'unto logike hadde *longe* ygo', it is reasonable to suppose that he had passed to the Quadrivium, i.e. to the study of arithmetic, geometry and astronomy (music seems to have been neglected), natural and moral philosophy—the distinction is still preserved in the names of two Oxford chairs—and metaphysics. This was essentially a course in the relevant works of Aristotle—or pseudo-Aristotle; and Dumbleton's *Summa* (of which two copies survive at Merton) was designed to cover the topics in the course on the physical sciences. Such works are evidence of the transition from pure scholasticism to natural science as we understand it; and it is in the light of this development that we should view Chaucer's choice of a central theme for his *Hous of Fame*. He could hardly have made that poetical survey of the starry regions and the laws of sound but for the impetus given by the Merton school. The eagle's discourse on sound waves (*HF* 765–803) follows closely the theory formulated by Grosseteste in his commentary on the *Posterior Analytics*, of which commentary Merton possessed four copies.

With all this Merton remained in tune with the dominant theology, and was not indifferent to literary studies: witness the names of Archbishop Bradwardine, Ralph Strode, and Bishop Reed. About Bradwardine a whole book and many papers have been written. Like Boethius, he was renowned as a mathematician as well as a philosopher (the Oxford course in mathematics was partly based on a summary of Boethius' *Ars Metrica*, the 'ars metryke' of the Summoner's Tale, D 2222); and his work *De proportionibus* is now seen to be significant for the development of mathematical physics. This is not the place, nor am I the proper man, to consider why Chaucer links Bradwardine's name with the discussion of the question

> Whether that goddes worthy forwiting
> Streyneth me nedely for to doon a thing   (*CT* B 4433–4)

or to ask whether Chaucer read Bradwardine's *De Causa Dei* before penning Troilus' soliloquy, or Arcite's, on free will; whether part of Wiclif's metaphysics may actually have derived (as Dr. Leff suggests) from Bradwardine;[1] or whether Langland's concern with predestination (*Piers Plowman* B x. 375 ff.) reflects Oxford controversies. The *De Causa Dei* (addressed *ad duos Mertonenses*) was evidently the outcome of a *disputacio* on the problem of free will as seen by yet another Mertonian, Thomas Buckingham, who had become fellow about the same time as Bradwardine, and was third bursar in 1358, a few years after Bradwardine left to join Richard of Bury's household. It is pleasing to think that such a subtle controversialist as Buckingham once checked college accounts or supervised harvests on the college fields at Holywell or Grantchester. Such a combination of diverse activities is characteristic of writers of the century (and pre-eminently of Chaucer). It has been one of the secrets of the abiding strength of Oxford as of Cambridge.

It is exemplified again in the career of Ralph Strode. The wording of Chaucer's request that Gower and Strode should, 'of youre benignites', correct his *Troilus* (*Tr.* v 1856–9) suggests that they were both not far away when he wrote it. In fact Strode had been given a *mansio* over Aldersgate at about the same time that Chaucer was leased his house at Aldgate, a few hundred yards off. Strode was then Common Serjeant, or pleader, of the City of London, and could have supplied several models for Chaucer's Man of Law from amongst his acquaintance. But before he became a lawyer he had been an eminent logician, Merton favouring the study of law less than logic. His *Consequentiae* and *Obligationes* were set texts at Padua in the fifteenth

---

[1] *Tr.* iv. 958 ('al that comth, comth by necessite') reads like a translation of Wiclif's '[nec] omnia que eveniunt de necessitate eveniunt' (Loserth, p. 181). H. Patch (*JEGP* xvii (1918), 417) compared *Tr.* iv. 1027 with a passage from *De Causa Dei*.

century—another indication of interchange between Oxford and Padua. Strode was just the man to spot errors in Chaucer's text (which certainly underwent revision) or in Troilus' logic; long after he had left Oxford he engaged in friendly disputation with a former Merton contemporary, John Wiclif, known in his day as a political and scholastic philosopher rather than as polemicist or crypto-Protestant; and Strode had associations with other Merton men after his city appointment.

Walter de Merton's intention was that fellows on his foundation should not remain all their lives at Oxford or become professional theologians or canonists: they were to serve God in Church or State—as he had done. What little we know of Strode suggests that he amply fulfilled this intention. His career ran in part parallel to Chaucer's, in philosophical temper he was akin to the poet. If we accept a fifteenth-century Mertonian's description he had poetic gifts himself: 'Nobilis poeta [qui] versificavit librum elegiacum, Phantasma Radulphi.' This poem has often been identified with the Middle English *Pearl*. But the *Pearl* is a *somnium*, conveying truth: it could never be called a *phantasma*, an illusory dream; and *liber elegiacus* may mean not an 'elegy', but a work in Latin elegiacs: in which case Chaucer very aptly links Strode with Gower, whose *Vox Clamantis* must be the longest work in elegiacs ever written. We should think of Chaucer, Gower, and Strode as a trio of accomplished London poets. Some manuscripts of the first (and later) recensions of Gower's massive *Confessio* conclude with complimentary Latin verses in near-Renaissance style by a certain philosopher (*quodam philosopho*), celebrating the completion of that little work (*opusculi*—a joke not approved by the scribe who changed the word in his copy to *operis*). 'Seagirt England,' claims this philosophical poet, 'echoing with your praise, sings far and wide your joyous verse. Honour, to you, poet, satirist and master of song; measureless is your renown.' Which seems to pick up Gower's own reference to Chaucer's 'ditees and songes glade', with which 'the londe fulfild is overal' (*Confessio* viii. 2945–7). If one version of the *Confessio* was finished by 1387, it is tempting to agree with G. C. Macaulay that *quidam philosophus* was the 'philosophical Strode' whose will (now lost) was proven in that year: though there are chronological difficulties in supposing that he was the same philosopher who composed the epilogue to Gower's *Vox Clamantis*, which can hardly have been finished before 1392. Similar difficulties arise if we accept as genuine the statement in one late manuscript of the *Astrolabe* that Strode was the tutor of 'little Lewis' Chaucer, who is described as ten years old in that text, i.e. in about 1391. Enough for our present purpose to note that from Strode and his Oxford friends Chaucer could have learnt most of what he needed to know about Oxford books, Oxford studies, Oxford life.

Students of Chaucer know of Strode, and students of metaphysics know of Bradwardine. But who knows of William Reed? Yet Reed was one of the brightest stars in all the Merton galaxy. As a book-collecting bishop he was the equal of Richard de Bury and of Balliol's later benefactor, William Gray. He shares the humanist interests of both; but his bequests and his own astronomical tables show that he was not indifferent to the scientific concerns of his Merton contemporaries. A biographer of Chaucer should note that Reed's patron was Nicholas of Sandwich, 'a leading man among the prosperous gentry of Kent', lord of two manors, but in orders. Sandwich proceeded M.A. in 1305 but he was living, and perhaps preaching, at Oxford as late as 1347; and it was perhaps at Oxford that he collected the astronomical, philosophical, and scientific works which he bequeathed to Reed, and which Dr. Emden conveniently lists for us. In 1358 Nicholas sold one of his manors at Bilsington to Edmund Staplegate; and in 1375 Chaucer acquired the wardship of Staplegate's son and heir, to whom two-thirds of this manor had descended. So Chaucer may at least have heard Sandwich's name. He certainly would have envied him his library.

Bishop Reed's bequest to Merton of over 112 books, together with a sum sufficient to build in 1375 the beautiful library that still stands in Mob Quad, gave Merton unchallenged pre-eminence as a centre of Oxford learning and, in Powicke's view, facilities almost as favourable as those at the Sorbonne itself. The gift marked the climax in a series of accretions that had been proceeding for nearly a century, ever since Archbishop Peckham, sometime Franciscan lector at Oxford, had, as Visitor, enjoined that three grammatical texts, and duplicates of any important works, should be chained in the library. But it is by the unchained books that we can best measure the library's growth. It was built up largely by gifts from former fellows: each being expected to bequeath his books, or to give them if he entered religion or took a post outside Oxford (many books came from bishops or canons who had thus 'made good')—or to give money in lieu. Thus William Burnell, dean of Wells from 1292 to 1295, left (*inter alia*) a Comestor and various works by Jerome including the *Contra Jovinianum* (the basis of part of the Wife of Bath's Prologue), and Henry de la Wyle, Senior Proctor in 1289, in 1329 bequeathed ten important manuscripts, including works of Aquinas and Aristotle. Chaucer's pilgrim-clerk, who yearned for twenty such books, would have had his heart's desire in Merton.

All these gifts added to the number of books which could be distributed to fellows for private study at the annual *electio*. It is this provision that made a fellowship so advantageous. And it is the four lists of books so distributed in the fourteenth century that enable us to reconstruct the contents of the early library; two were found by H. W. Garrod while exploring the attics at the head of his

staircase one snowy afternoon fifty years ago. On the list
for 1338, in the very heyday of the scientific movement, is
written the revealing complaint: 'Magistri qui non inten-
dunt physicis occupant libros philosophiae': that is: M.A.s,
though not reading for a degree, snap up all the scientific
books. But, thanks to donors, by mid century the library
had some 340 volumes (which meant many more than that
number of titles), of which about a tenth survive. They
range from Isidore of Seville's Encyclopedia and four fine
volumes of Vincent of Beauvais's *Speculum* (another work
on which the Wife of Bath's Prologue draws heavily) and
several copies of Seneca (see *CT* D 1183, 2018), down to
such monuments of English learning as the works of
Bradwardine and Bracton. The full extent of Reed's con-
tribution has only become known with the discovery of an
indenture of 1374, carefully grouping titles by categories.
The fact that a busy cleric should have read, and collected,
as widely as the lists indicate surely suggests that the
incipient humanism which Miss Smalley has detected in
the writings of Oxford friars earlier in the century was not
altogether abortive. It also suggests that Chaucer could
count on an audience, fit, if few, acquainted with such
works as the following—all found in Reed's list, and all
used, or alluded to by the poet:

'Books of Scipio and Macrobius'—i.e. Macrobius'
Commentary on Cicero's *Somnium Scipionis*, Chaucer's
'myn olde boke totorne'; Averroes and Avicenna (Chaucer's 'Avicen')—i.e. their Commentaries on Aristotle,
including Averroes's *De Caelo et Mundo*; Geoffrey of Vinsauf's *Poetria Nova* (Chaucer's 'Gaufred dere maister
sovereyn'); the *Legenda Sanctorum* (invoked by the Wife
of Bath); the *Historia Jerosolimita*—possibly that of
Josephus, Chaucer's 'Ebraik Josephus, the olde', of whose
history Merton already had one copy (MS. 317); the
Odes of Horace (echoes of which some critics have found
here and there in the Chaucer canon); Martianus Capella,

the 'Marcian' on whom the dreamer thinks in the *Hous of Fame* along with 'Anteclaudian' (in a Sorbonne manuscript the two texts are bound together, and perhaps Chaucer knew them so bound); the *liber Electionum* of Zahel, from which text is taken the marginal quotation in the Ellesmere and Hengwrt manuscripts opposite the Man of Law's question: 'Of voyage is ther non eleccioun?'; Innocent III's *De Miseria Humanae Condicionis*, which the same Man of Law paraphrases; Philip de Thaon's French Bestiary, a work that Chaucer probably knew in its Latin form since he calls it *Phisiologus* (*CT* B 4461); not to mention standard works by Augustine (who overtops all other authorities in the whole library), Bede, Boethius, Burley, Albert the Great, Peter de Riga; Gregory (including the *Moralia*), Bernard, Jerome—all three cited in any notes to the Parson's tale along with Peraldus, *De Viciis*, of which Merton also had a copy. In a different category are the works of Ptolemy and an exposition of the *Almagest* and other astronomical books. Amongst the 'legends, chronicles and histories' we note the (lost) *Vita S. Thomae Cantuariensis* ('peroptima') in no fewer than seven books: another sign of Oxford's devotion to that saint. The absence of Ovid and Virgil is not surprising when we recall that these were essentially school texts in the Middle Ages; but before 1410 Merton had a copy of Bersuire's influential commentary on the *Metamorphoses*, a work often appealed to in recent years by Chaucerian exegetes concerned with Chaucer's images and interpretations of pagan gods. A clerical secretary of Bradwardine's who should be honourably mentioned here gave to Merton the only copy of Marco Polo that reached Oxford in Chaucer's time, when copies were very rare anywhere in England—though some scholars think Chaucer had seen one.

It would be tedious, and possibly misleading, to pursue these correspondences: tedious because the list is long, and seriously misleading if I seemed to imply that Chaucer owed his knowledge of such works to Merton and that they were accessible to him there. My purpose is rather to suggest, first, that Reed's gifts to Merton, taken together with those to New College (fifty-eight manuscripts), Exeter (twenty-five), Balliol, Oriel, and Queen's (ten each), testify to a culture not very different from that in which fifteenth-century humanism was to flourish; secondly, that we gain something by envisaging the books that Chaucer knew not as separate and disparate items but as part of collections deliberately made and constantly used; and thirdly, that if we are to make any useful comments on Chaucer's learning we must find out what his acquaintances and other contemporaries read. The Merton lists give us as convenient and illuminating a cross-section as we can hope for. We cannot prove that Chaucer ever stepped inside the gates of Merton, still less that he knew of the college's literary resources from Strode or other Oxford acquaintances. All that we can say is that if he, or his 'little Lewis', did spend any time at Oxford, Merton must have been his Mecca. The holdings of books at St. Paul's school (which Chaucer may well have attended) are thin by comparison.[1]

There were, to be sure, greater libraries elsewhere—at Dover and Canterbury, at York and Bury (which could boast 2,000 volumes: no wonder Lydgate's learning rather overwhelmed him with such riches on his doorstep). Mr. J. H. Fisher thinks that Gower used books in the library at St. Mary Overy at Southwark; but Gower had a special association with that priory and not even Dr. Neil Ker can tell us whether such libraries were in general accessible to laymen. Again, there is no proof that Chaucer ever visited York or Bury, or even passed through

---

[1] They were published by Edith Rickert, *Modern Philology*, xxix (1931–2), 258–70; cf. her *Chaucer's World*, pp. 121–7. A catalogue of Oriel College Library made in 1375 occupies five printed pages (OHS v. 66) but is far shorter than the Merton lists.

Canterbury after that early journey in 1360. Dr. Emden has recently published a list of donors of books to St. Augustine's, Canterbury, to which Abbot Thomas Fyndon left several volumes.[1] Naturally several of the Merton titles recur in the Canterbury Catalogue, but one type of book that we do not find at Merton, and would not expect to find in a monastery, is liberally represented at Canterbury; by 1299 it had three volumes for leisure reading, including *Gui de Warwic*, and *c.* 1375, the year of Reed's bequest, a monk of the Abbey left it eleven volumes of romances—probably French, like *Le Chevalier au cygne*, known to have been in a monastic library about the same time. Such works had no place in a college collection; Chaucer himself had no great passion for French romances and he could have found what he needed of this kind in a London bookshop.

Of Reed's theological and philosophical texts (some probably going back to his student days) and of their associations with earlier Merton *alumni* I have neither time nor competence to speak. One of the most interesting Mertonian items in his library never reached Merton, but became MS. Digby 176 in the Bodleian. It contains as many as thirty-two articles, some bought from Bradwardine's executors, some in Reed's own hand. Amongst the latter are his calculations of the almanac of the sun *super meridiem Oxonie* for the years 1341–4, when he was an undergraduate or B.A.; there are notes by John Ashenden, the college's most renowned mathematician; and William Merle's *Regule ad Futuram Aeris Temperiem Pronosticandam*, which Nicholas the Oxford clerk who was consulted on such points (*CT* A 3196) would have found useful; Merle also left an account of the unhappy conjunction of Saturn, Mars, and Jupiter in 1367 (Digby 176, f. 40) by Reginald Lambourn, a fellow of Merton in the

---

[1] See A. B. Emden, *Donors of Books to S. Augustine's Abbey Canterbury* (Oxford Bibl. Soc., 1968), pp. 3–4.

fifties, who became a monk at Eynsham near by.[1] A Strode
nurtured in such a nest of astronomers and weathermen
would cast more than a cursory eye on the verse in the
Troilus beginning

> The bente mone with hir hornes pale
> Saturne, and Jove, in Cancro joyned were,
> That swich a rayn from hevene gan avale . . .
> *(Tr.* iii. 624–6)

Such conjunctions and their possible influences are the
actual theme of Ashenden's *Summa Judicialis de Accidentibus Mundi,* described in MS. Royal 12 F. xviii as 'tractatus
de significacione conjunccionis Saturni et Martis in Can-
cro que erit isto anno Christi 1357, 8° die et de significacione conjunccionis Saturni et Jovis que erit anno Christi
1365 in 30 die octobris hora 14 min. 29'.[2]

Reed's own learning in astronomy is evidenced by some
of the books that he bequeathed to Merton and that are
still there. One of these (A.3.9; Powicke 531; Coxe 35)
seems at first sight to be a typical medieval compilation:
including works by Augustine, Anselm, Hugh of St. Vic-
tor, Giles of Rome. But at the end are three astronomical
treatises:

1. A tract on the chilindrum [a portable cylindrical
dial] and the quadrant, of which the beginning is lost;
but it ends 'que composita fuit Oxonie'—like a similar
treatise in MS. Digby 98, 'quae facta est apud Oxoniam';
and the editor of Howden's *Practica Chilindri* suggests that
it too was composed for use at Oxford.[3] The name of

---

[1] Lambourne sent a table of eclipses to John of London at St. Augustine's,
which had other connections with Oxford; he noted earlier tables in several of
his books, including Bodl. MS. Rawl. C. 117, which includes a table 'ad
inveniendum lune equatorium'.

[2] Leland found a similar item at Peterhouse: *Collectanea* (1770), iv. 21 ff.
Similar calculations by Mauduit survive in C.U.L. MS. Gg vi 3, f. 45. (This
manuscript contains a work *de judiciis siderum* by *magister* Roger de Hereford
who is not listed in Emden's *BRUO* or *BRUC.*)

[3] See *Essays on Chaucer* (Chaucer Soc., 1868), Part I, no. 2.

Howden takes us back to an earlier century and an earlier science—the by no means negligible experimental science of Bishop Grosseteste, Oxford's first chancellor, the *philosophus* or *Lincolniensis* of many a marginal note. Howden can hardly have been at Merton, though a Merton man describes him a *dominus meus* and *beatus*: *beatus* because Howden, clerk in the service of Queen Eleanor, was also the author of the *Philomena*—that important link between Franciscan poetry and the English fourteenth-century mystics. What age later than the fourteenth century has produced a like combination of science and devotion?

Along with this tract Reed gave to Merton a *chilindrum* to use according to it. It has not survived, though there is a seventeenth-century example in the Ashmolean Museum. In the Shipman's Tale, that worldly monk 'my lord daun John' says, somewhat ostentatiously, 'by my chilindre it is pryme of day' (B 1396)—displaying his new and fashionable gadget. Chaucer thus anglicizes the term, and when Lydgate uses it later he is probably imitating his master.

2. Second in Reed's compilation comes a treatise on a new type of quadrant, popularized by Jacob ben Makir (Profacius) in the early fourteenth century. The instrument itself Reed also gave to Merton, where it can still be seen.

3. Third is a copy of Grosseteste's work on the sphere. Again Reed gave the instruments to accompany it—both a *spera solida* and a *spera materialis*; possibly the former was 'the solid sphere with a case' which appears on the Merton *electio* for 1410. Chaucer, in his treatise on the astrolabe, seems twice to refer to some previous account of the solid sphere (Part 1, para. 17; cf. II, para. 26), possibly written by himself; in which case he probably based it on Grosseteste's work, and probably himself owned a *spera solida* like Reed's. In so far as a work on the equatory, such as that in the Peterhouse manuscript edited by Dr. Price, would fit neatly into a series of tractates on sphere, astro-

labe, equatory, the case for ascribing the Equatory to Chaucer is slightly strengthened.

The manuscript we have been considering was one of several bought by Reed with money given him by Nicholas Sandwich, aforementioned. But we also find at Merton a book that Sandwich himself gave to Reed, viz. C.2.10, a collection of works of Arabic astronomy, including:

i. The tables and canons of al Zarqali, and the book on celestial motions of al Farghani, who figures as Alfraganus in Gower's *Confessio Amantis* (vii. 1461); Gower's knowledge of the literature of the subject seems to be sketchier than Chaucer's, since at the same place he cites as an 'auctor'—i.e. as an authority—

> Arachel, the which men note:
> His bok is Abbategnyh hote;

which appears to represent a confused recollection of two titles listed in Reed's bequest of books to Richard of Campsall (not the fellow of that name but the rector of St. Martin's Canterbury): viz. the *Centiloquium Beteni* (al Battani), and the *Canones Arzachelis* (al Zarqali). The names appear side by side in Reed's will, so perhaps the two books commonly went together, and perhaps Gower was miscopying from a list of such works—spoofing, in fact.

ii. John of Spain's translation of the 'Introduction to the Mystery of Judgements from the Stars' by Abdilazi—the Alchabitius of Chaucer's treatise on the astrolabe.

iii. The Liber Alkyndi (translated by Robert Chester), which is listed among Nicholas's possessions as 'the book that hight *non est judicium*' in the Paris manuscript extension of *CT* A 3209. (Manly and Rickert v. 319.)

iv. Another item in Sandwich's volume is the famous Tables of Toledo: *Tabulae Tholotanae de Cursibus Planetarum*: a name retained even when they were replaced by the Alfonsine tables compiled for Alfonso the Wise. No less than thirteen copies of these later tables are associated with Oxford, and the Merton School. It is by these 'tables Tolletanes' that the subtle clerk of Orleans (a university, be it noted, which attracted many English students)—more thorough than Nicholas, who is a typical Oxford amateur—works out his equations in the Franklin's Tale. His were 'ful wel corrected' (*CT* F 1274), i.e. for the longitude of Orleans. Reed himself prepared tables similarly corrected for the meridian of Oxford; several copies of these tables survive, giving tables of *anni collecti* and *anni expansi*—the clerk of Orleans's 'collect and expans yeres'.[1] His terminology is partly reminiscent of Reed's, partly of the treatises on the astrolabe and the equatory. The *Equatory* elucidates such terms of the Franklin's as 'centres' and 'arguments' and 'proportionels', 'his eighte spere in his wirking', and his 'equacions' (*CT* F 1276 ff.); 'Argument' in the Franklin's technical meaning is not found outside these three texts till 1796, and 'equacioun' again only in the astronomical sense in the *Confessio Amantis*—and there in a passage strikingly similar in application to the lines in the Franklin's Tale (vi. 1957 ff.). Conjoined with the Toledan Tables in Reed's manuscript are three Latin treatises on the astrolabe (f. 48, 89 ff.) which thus supplemented another work on this instrument that had been in the Merton Library for over a century; not to mention a cryptic reference in the earliest catalogue to *Martialis*—perhaps a disguised form of Maschala, or

---

[1] At least 10 Oxford MSS. contain tables based on the Oxford meridian: Bodl. 432 (f. 32ᵛ), Digby 10 (f. 9), 57 (ff. 119ᵛ ff., inc. 'tab eclipsium . . . 1376–89', 97 (f. 22), 98 (f. 162), 114 (f. 22), 176 (ff. 94 ff.), Laud Misc. 594 (f. 84) and 674 (ff. 67 etc.), Lyell 37 (pp. 25, 71: cf. p. 103 [l. xvc]), and Jesus Coll. 46 (f. 3). Two Oxford tables occur in C.U.L. MS. Ii i 27 (dated 1424), ff. 17ᵛ ('1348') and 19; this MS. also contains copies of two tables of William Reed's (ff. 7ᵛ, 15) (cf. N. R. Ker's account of the Royal Astronomical Society's MS. QB. 7/1021, *Medieval Manuscripts in British Libraries*, i (1969), 193) and Ashenden, *Summa Judicialis de Accidentibus Mundi* (ff. 61–140); for the use of Ashenden's work at Oxford see *Mediaeval Studies*, xxvi 1964), 173.

'Massahala', an authority on whom Chaucer drew for the *Astrolabe*.[1]

Merton was, indeed—and still is—an ideal place to study the astrolabe (it is not surprising that the most recent monograph on Chaucer's astronomy comes from that college). Even before 1325 it possessed two of these instruments, kept in leather cases: one of them perhaps being the 'astrolabium antiquum cum duplici rete' listed in the *electio* for 1452: the 'rete' is the open-work plate on the front of an astrolabe which in the English treatises on Astrolabe and Equatory is called a *riet*.[2]

Thus one by one every astronomical trail in Chaucer leads us to Oxford, and in Oxford to Merton. Whether 'litel Lowys' for whom he wrote his treatise on the astrolabe was fictional, illegitimate, a godson, or in some vaguer relation, the tables it refers to were 'compowned after the latitude of Oxenforde', and the promised tables of equations of the planetary mansions were likewise to be adjusted to that latitude. In view of the fact that so many astronomical tables were produced in Oxford, these references are not in themselves remarkable. But in showing how to establish the latitude Chaucer adds: '*wel I wot* the latitude of Oxenford is certain minutes lasse, *as I mighte prove*', which suggests that he is not merely translating an Oxford text. The *Astrolabe* of Chaucer itself became an Oxford text inasmuch as at least one copy of it (MS. Bodley 619) was made by an Oxford astronomer.

Again, the missing third part of Chaucer's treatise was to be based on 'the kalendres of the reverent clerkes, frere J. Somer and frere N. Lenne' (another indication that his opinion of friars should not be deduced solely from the

---

[1] For the ascription see *Medium Ævum*, xxxvii (1968), 233.

[2] There may be a reference to this term in the cryptic verses addressed to the chancellor of Oxford 1334/5, OHS n.s. iv. 110–11:

> Sidera seruasti, dum nos vis jungere mete;
> Nos conculcasti; modo frangitur a pede *rete*.

fictional tales). John Somer was at Greyfriars, Oxford from 1380 to 1395 or later, and two tables of his survive —one in the unique Peterhouse manuscript of the equatory itself: f. 63ᵛ of which has a list giving the true *motus* and ecliptic latitude for 31 December 1393, headed 'J. Somer Oxonia';[1] the other is a decemnovenal calendar for the period 1387–1462 'ad meridiem tamen univ. Oxonie'.[2]

This table Somer had made at the instance of the provincial of his order for Joan, Princess of Wales, mother of Richard II. The illuminated copy that is now Royal 2 B viii in the British Museum was doubtless the presentation copy, and if so would have been used by Richard, and quite possibly accessible to Chaucer. It was probably for such services that Somer received a royal grant in the same years that Chaucer did, namely 1399 and 1400 (and later). The occurrence of his name in both the *Astrolabe* and the *Equatory* is one of several indications that the latter was a sort of companion-piece to the former.

The other friar named by Chaucer, Nicholas of Lynn, or Lynn Episcopi, now King's Lynn, Norfolk, was an Oxford Carmelite, described by Bale as 'philosophus, cosmographus, et astronomicus inter omnes sui temporis celeberrimus' (Bale had been a Carmelite himself, and perhaps retained some vestiges of loyalty to his order). Nicholas likewise compiled a calendar for 1387–1462, and likewise for the Oxford meridian: a continuation of one made by 'reverendus magister Walterus Elveden', which was formerly in the library of Gonville and Caius, of which college Elveden had been a member and possibly a fellow;[3]

---

[1] A horoscope in the Peterhouse MS. has been adapted to the Oxford latitude.

[2] For extant copies see *BRUO*, s.v. Leland saw one at Clare Hall: and for a reference to Somer in MS. Laud 674 see *Studies Presented to Sir Hilary Jenkinson* (1957), p. 219 n. 1.

[3] See Emden, *Biographical Register of the University of Cambridge* (1963), s.v. Leland, who saw the Calendar at Gonville Hall, describes it as 'calendarium cum tribus cyclis decemnovalibus...'; Bale adds 'factum 1327', but that date seems

he was certainly an innovator in astronomical studies at Cambridge, and could have easily had contact with Nicholas: Cambridge being then accessible from Lynn by both road and river, and contacts between the two towns being close.[1] Lynn's table was made for John of Gaunt—a curious parallel, this, with Somers's, made for Princess Joan, and an indication of Gaunt's quasi-royal status—at a time when Philippa Chaucer was still connected with his household.[2] There is a strong likelihood that Chaucer used Nicholas's calendar for the calculations alluded to in the Nun's Priest's Tale and the Parson's Prologue.

Possibly Nicholas Lynn plays another part in our story. One of Dr. Price's achievements was to read under ultra-violet light some erased letters in the very first line of the *Equatory*: after the word *seyde* he made out 'leyk'—evidently intended for the name of the source or author of the text. The erasure suggests that the scribe miswrote the name, or that a corrector thought it wrong. Dr. Price believed it quite possible that the word is an error for 'Leyners' viz. John of Linières, a famous astronomer. It is equally possible that it is an error for Lenn (= Lynn), or that it represents another form of Lynn's name: for in Bodleian MS. Laud 662 a continuation of his calendar is ascribed to Nicholas de Leuka. I find a Robert de Leke in Cambridge documents, but no place of that name in Cambridgeshire. It may have been a small village,

---

too early. The MS. has disappeared, but the college has an early fourteenth-century astrolabe that may be Elveden's. Copies of the continuation by Nicholas 'de Leuka' are in MSS. Laud 662 and (incomplete) Soc. Ant. 8.

[1] Witness the story told by Bishop Brinton about a sailor from King's Lynn who used to bring letters by river from Brinton's friends; excommunicated by the Vice-Chancellor, he drowned himself 'circa Prestishouse': *The Sermons of Thomas Brinton*, ed. Mary Aquinas Devlin (1954), i. 134.

[2] 'Industrious' Hakluyt gratuitously identified 'N. Lenne' with an Oxford Franciscan astronomer who is said to have visited the Arctic regions in 1360. It is curious that the account of this journey is said to have been presented to the King of Norway by a priest who had an astrolabe (as if that object was a great rarity in northern parts).

Nicholas's birthplace, in the Lynn area. The *Leyk* of the *Equatory* and the *Lenne* of the *Astrolabe* may thus be one and the same authority.

Though references to the equatories of the planets are said to be not uncommon in medieval astronomical literature, the only descriptions I can find in English documents (outside the Peterhouse text) are in the Merton *electio* of 1410, which lists an *equatorium ligneum* (the English treatise says the instrument may be made either of metal or of board planed smoothly), and an *equatorium aeneum*—both with epicycles; the latter is perhaps the instrument described in the 1452 *electio* (no. 13) as 'cum epiciclo in dorso cum volvelles solis et lunae'.[1] But it was evidently different from the only extant medieval example of an equatory, which—one is hardly surprised to learn—is to be found on the back of a Merton astrolabe, and embodies improvements corresponding to the prescription given in the Peterhouse text, and given there only. The Merton instrument, says Dr. Price, also incorporates the primules for observational use prescribed by Richard of Wallingford. The only other mention of the instrument I know of is in the remarkable list of books and scientific instruments belonging to John Erghom (alias John of Bridlington) who had studied and taught at the Austin friars at Oxford before he became Prior of the York convent in 1385.[2] His two equatories were almost certainly acquired at Oxford: one is described as *equatorium abbreviatum cum canonibus Badcomb* (*abbreviatum*, I take it, means a smaller type than the one envisaged by the author of the *Equatory*, which was no less than six feet in diameter); the other is described as formerly belonging to Richard Thorpe, 'magister'. William Badcomb, or Batecomb, was an Oxford master whose astronomical tables for the latitude of Oxford, and per-

---

[1] For volvelles see R. T. Gunther, *Early Science in Oxford* (1920–45), ii. 235–41.

[2] See *Fasciculus J. W. Clark dicatus*, pp. 2–96.

petual almanac (*c.* 1248), are extant in Magdalen College
MS. 182; and Thorpe is probably the fellow of Queen's
who according to notes on the margin of Royal MS. 12 D
vi (ff. 7–50) calculated the latitude of London. The same
manuscript contains tables Thorpe drew up in York for
the year 1392 (the year to which our Equatory belongs);
they refer to Simon Bredon's tables (1356) for the latitude
of Oxford. It also contains Reed's adaptation of the
Alfonsine tables to the meridian of Oxford (f. 27^v); an
earlier table for the years 1387–1418; and a tantalizing
fragment (f. 81^v) of a Middle English version of a table
of 'assenciouns of the signes by 6. houses for the latitude
51° 50'', 'as is precisely ynow3 for Oxenford'. The writer
calls himself Walter Anglus and a scribe adds that he
flourished *c.* 1400, and was educated at Winchester and
Coll. B. Marie Virg. Oxon. (viz., New College). He was
in fact a fellow of that college.

Yet another item in the Royal manuscript indicates
Oxford's priority, and Merton's influence, in astronomical
studies. It is a note saying that a set of Cambridge tables
were carefully checked in 1406 by five Cambridge men—
'per quinque homines valde morose atque deliberate
operantes in universitate Cantabrigie'—using two copies
of the Alfonsine tables, two of John of Linières, four
of 'Magister Willelmus Reede', and one of Magister
Johannes Mauduit, with whom my tale began. The tables
the Cambridge men were using were presumably those that
Mauduit had composed in Oxford a century before (1310),
of which copies survive (in Laud Misc. 674 ff. 69–72 and
C.U.L. Gg vi 3). That these five 'studious and deliberate'
men stimulated others to astronomical study is indicated
by a donation to Peterhouse, about a century after Reed's
bequest to Merton, of 'tabulae equacionum planetarum
magnae'—which may well be a description of the English
equatory manuscript, measuring as it does fourteen by
eleven inches; along with it went two items that Merton

had acquired long before: (i) the *Perspectiva Whitelonis*—a translation of the Optics of Ibn al Haitham (Alacen)—which was at Merton before 1325, though later lost, to be replaced by two others; and (ii) Albert the Great's *Historia Animalium*, which came to Merton *c.* 1385 and is still there (O.2.2). Thus even Cambridge evidence works in favour of Oxford's precedency in science.[1]

We may come down from the country of the stars, from the galaxy that Chaucer liked to think of as a heavenly Watling Street, and back to the concerns of the Canterbury pilgrims, by way of one last astronomical item culled from the Merton library. The very first catalogue (*ante* 1325) includes the basic text for all mathematical and astronomic study: the *Megiste Suntaxis Astronomias* of Claudius Ptolemaeus: the *Almagest*, as it became known when an Arabic translator added the Arabic article to *megiste*. Reed had his own copy—but gave it to Exeter, presumably because Merton by this time had two. And the Wife of Bath can plausibly cite it—or rather, Gerard of Cremona's preface to his Latin version—because it is just the kind of text that Jankin, her fourth husband, if lately come from Oxford, would quote at her:

> Whoso that nil be ware by othere men,
> By him shul othere men corrected be:
> The same wordes writeth Ptholomee;
> Rede in his Almageste, and take it there.
>   (D 179–83; cf. 324–5)

That Jankin's wife took note of what he read she later in her prologue makes quite plain. Most of the 'Romayn geestes' and *exempla* that Jankin appealed to he found in Valerius Maximus (not a 'schools' text, but Merton acquired a Commentary on it, after Chaucer's time) and

---

[1] In 1417 Peterhouse also acquired a MS. of John Ashenden's *Summa* (now Royal Coll. Physicians, MS. 390). Peterhouse MS. 250, which includes a tract 'De spera', and notes 'de opere chilindri' and 'nomina parcium astrolabii', did not reach the library till the eighteenth century.

Jerome's *contra Jovinianum*, which had the prestige of a
patristic text and appears, like the *Almagest*, in the first
Merton catalogue. The Merton copy is bound up with
some twenty-four other patristic items, together with one
of much later date, based on Grosseteste's notes on the
Nicomachean Ethics: a more likely combination than Jankin's 'omnibus', which included

> the Parables of Salomon,
> Ovydes Art [of Love] and bookes many on,
> And alle this wer bounden in o volume.
>
> (D 679 ff.)

But since the Merton volume has over 350 folios, Jankin's
is not quantitatively implausible; at Merton the *Parabole
Salamonis* were bound up with the book of Job: a work
equally helpful for the husband of such a wife.

The Wife at first characterizes her Jankin as not only
'joly' but also 'hende': he has the polish of an educated
man. To Harry Bailly an Oxford education means the
polish of rhetoric: he begs the clerk to spare them the
'terms', 'colours', 'figures', and reserve the high style for
letters to kings:[1]

> Speketh so pleyn *at this tyme*, we yow preye,
> That we may understonde what ye say.
>
> (E 19–20)

But the clerk ignores the soft impeachment. To him
Petrarch is dear for his 'rhetoric sweet', and he flourishes
the rhetorical term *prohemium* before us. Curiously
enough, Professor Murphy, who has devoted an article to
Rhetoric in fourteenth-century Oxford, ignores the implications of this passage, and implies that the study of
rhetoric was not taken seriously till the fifteenth century.[2]
But Merton library had not only copies of the ancient

---

[1] *CT* E 31–5: where 'other art particuler' has a flavour of the Schools (cf.
F 1132); Chaucer's is much the earliest use of the phrase in English. I have not
traced any early MSS. of Petrarch or Legnano to Oxford; but Merton had
a copy of Alderotti, a 13th-century teacher at Bologna, the 'Ippocratista' of
Dante's *Paradiso*, xii. 83.   [2] *Medium Ævum*, xxxiv (1965), 1–20.

rhetorical texts—Donatus and Priscian (Reed had his own copy of Cicero *De Rhetorica*)—but also the popular *Grecismus* of Eberhard of Bethune, probably the *Doctrinale* of Alexandre de Ville-dieu, and certainly Geoffrey of Vinsauf. Instruction in writing letters to kings, popes, and bishops was part of the *ars dictaminis*. Whatever the place of that art in the curriculum of the schools and the grammar schools (or the 'business schools'), the fourteenth-century formularies edited by Salter indicate that it was extensively practised by Oxford men from Richard of Bury onwards; and Dr. Schoeck has shown that in fact all the English dictaminal treatises from 1220 to 1450 are connected with Oxford. If Chaucer did not have this association in mind it is hard to see why the Host alludes to the epistolary style at all. But the character assigned to clerks most often in the Tales, and, we must suppose, in the popular mind, was subtlety, and preternatural cleverness, sometimes associated with astronomical, sometimes with argumentative skill. (Deschamps defines the Logic of the *Trivium* as 'après une science d'arguer choses faintes et subtiles . . .')[1] Almost the first thing that 'hende' Nicholas says is:

> A clerk hadde litherly biset his whyle
> But if he koude a carpenter bigyle.
>
> (A 3299–30)

Simkin puts the Cambridge clerks' cunning ('queinte crekes') down to their philosophical training: he will fool them 'for al the sleighte in her philosophye' (A 4050). And when the Squire wishes to emphasize the false tercelet's casuistry he says that no one could 'countrefete the sophimes of his art' (F 553–4); whilst the Host accounts

---

[1] *L'Art de Dictier*, vii. 266–7. This is the 'subtilite of speche' that Chaucer's eagle disavows, along with 'gret prolixite / of termes of philosophie' (*Hous of Fame* 855–7): an early fifteenth-century *disputacio* (Magd. Coll. Ox. MS. 38) begins: 'Ne verborum prolixitas venerabili auditorio inferat fastidium . . .'; in fact it shows a liberal use of the 'colours of rhetorike' that the eagle likewise disavows.

for the Oxford clerk's silence by saying 'I trowe ye studie about some sophyme' (E 5). All these comments bear witness to the effect on the popular mind of the reorientation of university studies that the rediscovery of Aristotle had brought about. All the philosophers and scientists I have mentioned had been trained in Aristotelian logic. Some of them—Bradwardine, Buckingham, Dumbleton, Heytesbury, Swineshead—were amongst its greatest exponents; and that they had predecessors at Merton we know from titles of works now lost. Heytesbury's *Regulae Solvendi Sophismata* is a characteristic product of the school.[1] *Sophismata logicalia*, fine-spun and subtle arguments, employed originally in an academic context as a formal display of ingenious reasoning, undoubtedly bred that delight in specious argument for its own sake which characterizes the later fourteenth century (and the Pandarus who can 'so wel and formaly arguwe': *Tr.* iv. 497). It colours most pictures of a 'clerk', and most applications of clerkly language—even in such a context as the Pardoner's account of cooks who 'turnen substaunce into accident' (C 539). Hence, ultimately, the plain man's suspicion of all learning as having to do with the arcane, the mystifying, the magical: Jankin's wife claims that he has *enchaunted* her. The suspicion was reinforced by that penchant of Arts men for the fashionable hobby of astrological prognostication—as with Nicholas—or for 'magik naturel'—as with the young clerks of Orleans in the Franklin's Tale (F 1120 ff.), where the suggestion clearly is that whatever their professional training they devoted their spare time to astrology: Aurelius' brother comes across a book of astrology on the desk of a bachelor of law. Now we shall find reason to think that Chaucer's Cambridge clerks may likewise have been law students; and

---

[1] Cf. Weisheipl in OHS n.s. xvi. 244. Robert Stonham (see p. 17 above) abbreviated Heytesbury's work: see Emden, *BRUO*, s.v. For *sophismata* see *Mediaeval Studies*, xxvi. 177.

Simkin may be quipping not only at their argumentative
skill, but at the clerkly pastime of natural magic when
he says:

> Lat se now if this place may suffise,
> Or mak it rowm *with speche*, as is youre gise.
>
> (A 4125–6)

Certain it is that the fashion for astrology (to be distinguished from the scientific studies I have touched on)
led to learning being identified with the art of creating
appearances, and something more than the stage devices
of 'tregetours': Aurelius' brother says:

> For with an *apparence* a clerk may make
> To mannes sighte that all the rokkes blake
> Of Britaigne were yvoyded everichon.
>
> (F 1157–9)

All he needed to do, of course, was to study the mansions
of the moon (F 1285–90) which causes the high tides that
in Brittany have unusually long periods of *détente*, and
ensure that Aurelius or Dorigen should visit the coast at
the right times.

And it was not only astrology and philosophy that were
suspect. John the carpenter says:

> Men sholde nat knowe of Goddes privetee.
> Ye, blessed be alwey a lewed man,
> That noght bot only his bileve kan!
>
> (A 3454–6)

—every phrase there smacks of contemporary distrust of
school divinity: 'Whereto', asks the poet of the Vernon
lyrics,

> Wharto wilne we forte knowe
> The poyntes of Goddes privetee?
> More then him lustes forte schowe
> We schulde not knowe, in no degre.
> And idel bost is forte blowe [blossom out]
> A Mayster of Divinite:

The more we trace the Trinite
The more we falle in fantasye;[1]

so the carpenter thinks Nicholas has fallen 'in som wod-
ness'—a charge that Nicholas inverts when he attributes
John's disaster to his own 'fantasye' (A 3835, 3840).
'Leve we ure disputisoun', the Vernon poet continues,
referring to the academic *disputaciones* on such topics, 'and
leeve on Him that al hath wrought.'

When al ur bokes ben forth brought,
And al ur craft of clergye
And al ur wittes ben thorw-out souȝt
Ȝit we fareth as a fantasye.

It is the very language Langland uses when speaking of
clerks who 'tell of the Trinity a tale or twain and 'bring
forth a bald [trite] reason', and 'put forth a presumption to
prove the Truth'. 'God is much in the gorge of these great
Masters [of the Schools]'—but Langland dismisses them
in the same breath with 'Munde the miller of *multa fecit
deus*' (*Piers Plowman*, B x. 44 ff.). Whatever the precise
implications of the phrase, the contempt is unmistakable.
How millers had come to earn such misliking the Reeve's
Tale will tell us.

[1] *Religious Lyrics of the Fourteenth Century*, ed. Carleton Brown (1924), p. 163.
Cf. *The Oxford Book of Medieval English Verse*, ed. Celia Sisam (1970), p. 478.
In the *Ludus Coventriae* the worldly learning of clerks, identified with that of
the Doctors in the Temple, skilled in dialectic, sophistry, physics, astronomy,
calculation, and necromancy, is set at nought by the child Jesus (EETS E.S.
cxx, p. 178).

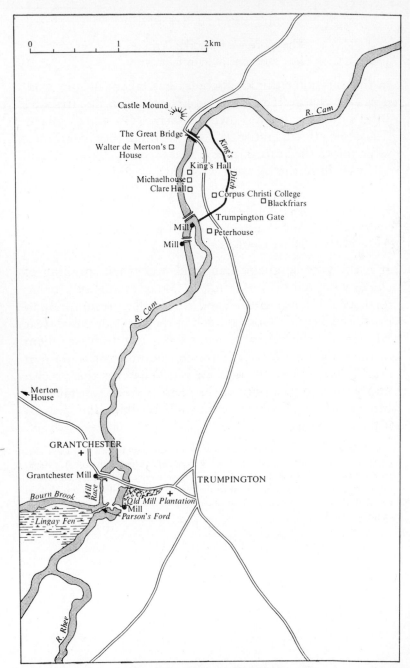

Fig. 3. Cambridge and Trumpington

IV

A JOLLY MILLER

In considering the story by which a carpenter takes
revenge for his craft on a miller we should keep in mind
that it was a reeve's tale. Of the Reeve described in the
Prologue we need for the moment recall only that 'wel
koude he kepe a garner and a bin' and reckon the increase
of his seed and grain, and that he rode 'a ful good stot /
That was al pomely grey, and hiȝte Scot' (which remained
a favourite East Anglian name for a horse until this century). No other horse in the cavalcade is so particularized.
Always in the saddle, the Reeve himself talks—to use
Chaucer's own epithet—in 'horsly' terms: 'grastime is
doon, my fodder is now forage' (A 3868); 'and yet ik have
alway a coltes tooth' (3888). According to Walter of Henley the reeve had to answer for the issue of the mares of the
manor. This is the very man to relish the spectacle of the
clerks' 'capul' running madly after the wild mares while
they shout and whistle after it: 'Keep, keep, stand, stand,
jossa! War þe rere!' (4101). His name (Oswald) like his
horse's, carries a suggestion of the North,[1] reinforced by
the northern pronoun in the first phrase he utters: 'So
thee'k'. It distinguishes him as a man able to reproduce
the dialect of clerks who came from Strother 'fer in the
north, I kan nat telle where'—and nor, precisely, can
anyone.

The Reeve himself comes from Bawdswell, in Norfolk,
some fifty miles north of Trumpington; so he might use,
on occasion, the form *melle* (3923) instead of *mille*; the

[1] The life of this Northumbrian saint was written by a Cambridgeshire monk
at Ramsey Abbey.

name Long Melford reminds us that -e- forms were common in East Anglia and they occur in Cambridge records
of the period.[1] He is the kind of man whose business might
well draw him to Trumpington Mill or Cambridge market; and I suggest that Chaucer names Bawdswell as nail-
ing him down to a particular part of Norfolk that puts him
within easy reach of these two places: within very easy
reach if he went by Lynn rather than Norwich. The village
is not quite as remote as editors give out. It is on the road
that would take Margery Kempe and many other pilgrims
(though not many like her) from Lynn to Norwich and
thence to East coast ports. Lynn Episcopi (as it was then
called) had trade connections with the north, and northern
works were probably read there.[2]

Even now, there is little difference between the West
Norfolk and the Cambridgeshire scene; and what can be
learnt from records about Cambridgeshire reeves neatly
fills out the sketch of the Reeve in the General Prologue.
A few miles away from Trumpington lies the village of
Great Shelford, in the fourteenth century a manor belonging to the rich abbey of Ely; and it is Ely records that
supply illuminating detail.[3] The office of reeve was in
theory one for which all customary tenants were liable, and
no salary attached to it beyond relief from customary
works, the right to eat at the lord's table at harvest-time,
and a few 'perks' such as forage for his horse when he rode
in his lord's duty; and sometimes (as in Fen Ditton, not

---

[1] Cambridge Guild records regularly have *melle(re)*; a Grantchester terrier
of *c.* 1440 (BM Add. Ch. 41415) has *le melle way*. The MS. of *CT* in Camb.
Gg iv 27 (which includes a picture of a jaunty Reeve in blue gown and red
stockings) has *melle(re)* throughout. This MS. has other marked East Anglian
features. Lydgate (Bury St. Edmunds) uses *melle* within a line: 'This greyn was
to the melle brought' (*Pilgrimage* 5422).

[2] A fifteenth-century letter from Lincs. to a correspondent living in or near
Lynn refers to 'ane Inglische buke es cald Mort Arthur': *Medium Ævum* xxxvii
(1968), 347.

[3] See Edward Miller, *The Abbey and Bishopric of Ely* (1951). I have drawn on
this work in the following sentences.

far from Trumpington) the right to put four ploughbeasts
into his lord's pasture; in Langland stots as well as oxen
serve as plough-beasts—so the Reeve, like the Ploughman,
is riding a working horse. He might also have half an acre
of wheat and barley, which he, like the Cambridge clerks,
would have to get a miller to grind. Place-names like
Reepham, Revesham, Reevesmead, suggest that he sometimes had a water-meadow also. In return, he had to collect
the rents due from the manor, transmit them to his lord,
dispense the customary liveries of food to the manorial
famuli and to boon workers at harvest-time, and pay any
wages that had to be paid, besides seeing that all plough-
beasts were in good condition. He was responsible for the
issue of grain, and sold what was surplus both of grain and
livestock; 'the garner and the bin' (593), the seed and
grain of the Prologue, were not actually his, but his lord's:
he had to see that no 'heaped measures' were taken from
grange to garner, and that surplus seed corn was returned.
Each year he had to present a compotus or roll for audit:
hence the force of the line in the Prologue: 'Ther was
noon auditour coude on him wynne' (594).[1]

When we consider that all these duties were discharged
by necessity rather than by choice, and that reeves were so
closely watched by auditors on the one side, and on the
other by their neighbours whose work they had to supervise—and who might speak up in the manor court against
them—it is not surprising that Chaucer depicts his reeve
as thin, worn, tetchy, and uncompanionable. Nor is it
surprising that when a suitable man had been found for
the job he tended to hold it for several years (as happened
at Great Shelford)—to become, in fact, a professional.
Years of watching for just such trickery as Miller Simon

---

[1] Auditor and reeve are similarly connected in *Piers Plowman*:

I halde it riȝte and resoun of my reue to take
Al that myne auditour, or elles my stuwarde
Conseilleth me by her accounte, and my clerkes wrytynge. (B xix. 457–9)

practises would leave him with no illusions about millers, but with some jealousy. The matching of the pair is deliberate: both are countrymen, of country thought and habit and concerns. Every other line of Oswald's description of Simkin glances at Robin the miller of the Prologue, who has been presented in purely farmyard terms; big of brawn, with beard red as any sow, and the hair on his wart 'red as the bristles of a sowes eres'. 'Drunk as a sow' ran the medieval proverb; and Robin when drunk snorts like one (3138). Simon gets himself into the same state: 'Swineshead', which clerk Aleyn mistakenly addresses to clerk John, fits the drunken miller, whom Aleyn has seized in the dark (4261), better than Aleyn knew. The country images the reeve finds for his own case are equally revealing: he is like a medlar, rotting 'in mullock or in stree' (3873): 'mullock' (rubbish) being an earthy dialect word, rarely evidenced in literature. His 'gras time is doon' is more than an old man's sigh: it carries the sexual sadness of the Wife of Bath's lament (D 477–8) that

> The flour is goon, ther is namore to telle;
> The bren, as I best kan, now most I selle;

while at the same time it suggests that Oswald finds a surrogate in the lusty coupling of horse and mare, Malin and Aleyn, the miller's wife and John.

It is just such an official as a reeve who would add to the usual taunts about a miller's dishonesty the different charge that he was a 'market-betere atte fulle' (3936). 'Market-beater', 'market-dasher' (which one manuscript reads), 'street-beater' are favourite terms of abuse in Wiclifite writings, though the contexts are not enlightening. One Wiclifite tract describes fourteenth-century hippies as 'yonge children' who 'wol not bisien hem to lerne, but bete stretes up and doun and synge and play as minstrelles and use vanytes and ydelnesse'. But another passage suggests a more deliberate activity; it denounces

a prelate or curate who flatters a lord or jumped-up gentle-
man 'though he be a marketbetere, a merchant or mayn-
teyner of wronges at lovedaies, a fals swerer, a manqueller'.[1]
I take it that the Miller is always ready to throw his weight
about in the goings-on at market, whether they be quarrels
or corners in wheat. In any event the main point of the
tale is that this market-beater whom no man durst touch
'for peril' is himself soundly beaten: 'Thise clerkes bete
him weel and lete him lye' (4308); which gives point to
the early emphasis on his prowess as a wrestler. Millers,
their muscles being daily flexed by hauling heavy sacks of
grain, have probably always been renowned for 'wrastling'
(3938). The only old-style miller I know used to go miles
to compete in 'wrastling matches' (his form) and still holds
them in his meadow.

Again it is the reeve from Norfolk who indicates his
Miller's standing in the country by saying, if with a sneer:

> grete soken hath this miller, out of doute,
> with whete and malt of al the land aboute. (3987–8)

Though *sac* and *soke* are familiar feudal terms in East
Anglia, *soken* is here used in a special technical sense:
meaning the exclusive right claimed by a mill-owner to
grind and take toll of all the grain of a manor or town in
which it stands. Such a right usually belonged to the lord
of the manor. But this is the late fourteenth century and
times are changing: the miller or his predecessor could
well have bought the freedom of the mill.[2] *Soken*, in the

---

[1] EETS o.s. 74, p. 242; cf. p. 172, and *Piers Plowman* B iii. 157; see J. W.
Bennett, *Speculum*, xxxiii (1958), 351–70.

[2] At his death in 1289 Roger de Trumpington held a mill (presumably that
at Trumpington) of one Simon de Cayli: W. Farrer, *Feudal Cambridgeshire*
(1920), p. 223. I cannot trace the tenancy in the 14th century. The mill may
have been farmed. If the miller had been the servant of the manor he would have
received a regular stipend. The nuns of Catesby (Northants.), who received tolls
of grain in kind from their mill, gave a certain proportion to the miller for his
household, as well as paying him a wage of 20s. and his servant 2s. 6d.: E. Power,
Medieval English Nunneries (1922), p. 107 n.

sense 'district', is largely East Anglian, as the place-
names Walsoken and Eaton Socon (some twenty miles
west of Cambridge) remind us.[1] 'Messuages', too, (3979)
would be part of the daily thought of a reeve; and his
reference provides much the earliest occurrence of the
term in English. It would be rash to attach importance to
the Reeve's use of Symkyn (3941, etc.) as a variant of
Symond (the only form used by the scholars); but Symkin
was certainly used in East Anglia.[2]

In the Reeve's part of England, as in the Cambridge
district, demesne farming was still the rule, and cereals
were still the main product, a good part going to the lord
of the manor. One of the reeve's jobs was to dispatch flour
or malt to the manor house or other residence; another
was to see to the repair or even rebuilding of his lord's
mills, using timber from his manors: another occasion
when miller and reeve would perforce have dealings.
Contemporary contracts tell us exactly how much rebuilding was done, how long it took, and how much it
cost. One of them names as the builder Henry Yevele,
by far the most famous of fourteenth-century builders,
who worked under Chaucer's direction and whose wages
Chaucer paid.[3]

A reeve, then, especially if, like Oswald himself, 'of
carpenter's craft', would have inside knowledge of mills
and millers. But what could be he expected to know of
a Cambridge college? Just so much as is set down in the
tale—which is more than may at first appear. Consider
what we are told:

---

[1] Langland has 'Rainalde the reve of Rotland Sokene' (*Piers Plowman* B ii.
110), Rutland being on the very edge of the area; the alteration in C to *Banne-
buries sokne* is suspect. *Soc* in the different sense of 'joint use of commons' is
similarly limited to Norfolk, Hunts., the Isle of Ely, and the valley of the Cam.
The Latin equivalent *luecia* / *luitia* is found only in Norfolk documents.

[2] *John of Gaunt's Register* (Camden Soc., 1937), i. 119.

[3] See John H. Harvey, *Henry Yevele* (1944). For some informative references
to work done by him see *BPR* iv. 247 (and other refs. in Index thereto).

i. That there was a great (some MSS. say 'fayre') college called the Soler Hall (3990).

ii. The head of the college was called a warden (4006, 4112).

iii. It provided board and lodging for young scholars, some of whom came from the north (4014–15) and are described in some manuscripts as 'poor'.

iv. It had a manciple (3993).

v. Its wheat and malt were ground at Trumpington Mill (3991).

vi. The college had a horse that carried sacks back and forth from Cambridge to Trumpington (4017).

I take these points in order.

i. In fourteenth-century Cambridge there was one college which though not 'great' (or 'fair') in the sense that King's, John's, or Trinity were to be, was certainly greater than other foundations then existing. This was the *Aula Regis*, or King's Hall. Its buildings were not as impressive as Merton's in Oxford. But it had a certain prestige as a royal foundation: its head was appointed by the Crown, and each fellow was appointed by writ under the Privy Seal. It had grown out of an 'experimental' society of King's scholars founded by Edward II, and reconstituted in 1330 as a *collegium* (a term first applied to Merton, fifty years before). Its purpose was to provide recruits for the civil service.[1] In a royal grant of 1342, in which the King appropriated to his Cambridge scholars the advowson of

---

[1] Several examples of wardens or fellows who entered the royal service in Chaucer's lifetime, including Nicholas of Drayton, rector of St. Martin's in the Vintry (for which see *Chaucer Life-Records* (1966), p. 12 n.), Richard Ronhale, Ralph Selby, and Richard de Medford, are given by Alan Cobban, *The King's Hall* (1969), Ch. 7.

Great St. Mary's (which was to serve for a century as the college chapel) it is called 'this great hall' (*tante sale*). It was great in another sense, too. There were seven or eight other foundations in existence before the end of the fourteenth century, but they had only about a dozen fellows each. Like the comparable Oxford institutions, they were essentially small graduate societies (of a pattern that both universities have reverted to 600 years later). The King's Hall, on the other hand, had 32 members in 1337, was enlarged to accommodate four more in 1342, and in 1375 embarked on a new extension which was still not complete when in September 1388 parliament met at Cambridge, or rather at Barnwell Abbey, just outside, where Richard II took up residence. Chaucer, a member of the previous parliament of 1386, was not re-elected to this one. He was at this time a Justice of the Peace for Kent. One of the important enactments of the Cambridge parliament limited the number of such Justices in each county to six, and when the new commissions were issued in July 1389, Chaucer's name was omitted. The proceedings at Cambridge would doubtless attract his attention to that town, even if he had no occasion (and he might well have had occasion) to visit it while parliament was in session. Its members were actually entertained at King's Hall, and at that time at least, the royal foundation would take on a certain reflected glory.[1] Its very existence as such a foundation probably encouraged the establishment of other colleges and so did something to redress the balance between Oxford and Cambridge.

Now editors state firmly that 'Soler Hall' was another name for the King's Hall. But in fact this name is not found in a single King's Hall document—nor in any other Cambridge record. On the other hand at least two buildings at Oxford, presumably once used as academic halls of

---

[1] See E. P. Kuhn, *PMLA* xxxvii (1922) 123.

the usual impermanent type, did bear this name.[1] This in itself disposes of the temptation to adopt the reading 'scoler hall' of some manuscripts: plausible at first sight but an obvious *facilior lectio* error, providing a quite non-distinctive description, since all colleges were 'scholars' halls'—hence we read of 'the scholars of the house of St. Peter', 'the scholars of the Hall of the University' (the predecessor of Clare Hall), etc.; Corpus was *domus scholarium Corporis Christi et B.V.M.*[2] 'Soler hall', on the other hand, has precedent in such names as Oriel Hall, Gutter Hall, Tyled Hostel, Chimney Hall, Coped Hall, and Garret Hostel—all named after an architectural feature. But why did Chaucer, using the term 'soler' (upper room) for the first time in English verse, apply it to a Cambridge college?

Because, perhaps, that college was distinguished by the number of solars it contained. It began in a house in Conduit lane formerly owned by one John Croyland: a thatched wooden building forming three sides of a court, with two floors on each wing, the upper consisting of solars, the ground floor of 'cellars':[3] the Hengwrt manuscript actually reads 'seler hall' but that probably reflects mere scribal uncertainty. There were thirteen rooms all

---

[1] See OHS lxviii. 182, 183, and lxxxix. 350 (this Soler Hall became Sorrel Hall, which stood on the site of Christ Church's Peckwater Quadrangle). For that in the parish of St. Peter in the East see lxxxv. 232, 441 etc.

[2] Cf. *Cambridge Gild Records, sub annis* 1344, 1349; *domus* is the term used in the accounts of an early pre-collegiate Oxford house: see *Oxoniensia,* xxxi. 81. For the terms *domus* and *aula* in Cambridge see H. E. Malden, *Trinity Hall* (1902), p. 3; Trinity Hall is still, familiarly, 'the Old House', as Christ Church is 'the House'; and the Merton toast is: *stet fortuna domus.* Queen's was still known as Queen's Hall in the sixteenth century: OHS xcii. 47. *Aula sive collegium Oriel* is at least once called 'the college of the King's Hall' (OHS lxxxv. 255; cf. lxvi. 177). On the other hand *novum collegium S. Marie Winton* (so called in 1392: OHS lxviii. 85: cf. lxvi. 387) is never called a hall.

[3] See Willis and Clark, *Architectural History of . . . Cambridge* (1886), ii. 431 ff. Cf. the description of Hart Hall, leased from Oseney Abbey by University College in 1353: 'continens unam aulam et sex cameras viz. tria solaria et tria cellaria': OHS lxxxix. 329.

told, in the original hall, two or more scholars living in each room, with as many as six in one. The clerks of the tale show that intimacy which chambering or chumming together would produce, and which has always been a feature of Cambridge life. There is no trace at King's Hall of the arrangement found at Peterhouse and elsewhere by which a junior member shared a room with a senior *in loco parentis*. Only the head of the house had a *camera* and a *studium* to himself. One of the rooms was known as the great solar; and the new building begun in 1375 included a large solar.

Solar, then, would be an apt, yet non-committal epithet to apply to the King's Hall. Chaucer seems almost to imply that it is not the official name when he says 'men clepen'— people *call* it the Solar Hall (3990); so an Oxford will speaks of *collegium regis vocatum Oriol*. The poet thus avoids any risk of libel; and the occurrence of the name Solar Hall at Oxford, if known, would assist the obfuscation, as does the variation between 'hall' and 'college'. In the King's Hall records *aula*, *sale*, *collegium* are used indiscriminately. This is in fact much the earliest recorded instance of 'college' as an English term.

In short, as Tyrwhitt said in another context, it is 'a designed misrepresentation'. The King's Hall was not so great that its members past or present would be above taking umbrage at a story which shows two of them in a risible situation. And in blending Oxford and Cambridge allusions Chaucer would merely be anticipating what Charles Lamb was to do in a once well-known essay on Oxford in the Vacation. That essay was actually written in Cambridge, though Lamb purports to be in rooms facing the Bodleian, and to find his friend, George Dyer (of Emmanuel, Cambridge) busy at Oriel (Oxford). Indeed Lamb, who ponders in a college kitchen on 'spits that have cooked for Chaucer', and who so hallows its meanest minister that the cook 'goes forth a manciple', evidently had the Reeve's tale in mind as he wrote: not surprisingly, since the road to Trumpington ran past his lodgings.

ii. The college has a warden, not a *magister* or a *praeses* or a *rector*. In the King's Hall Statutes and records the usual description of its head is *magister sive custos* (master or warden) indicating that no special importance attached to the title, though the letters patent issued to Bishop Arundel in 1383, when conducting an inquiry, say simply *custos*. It seems doubtful whether members of any other Cambridge college would call its head 'warden'. Indeed the *Oxford English Dictionary*, astonishingly, gives no citation before 1576—not even this one. At Oxford, on the other hand, *custos* was the only term recognized at Merton, the oldest foundation, and William of Wykeham adopted it for his new college (and new school).[1] If Chaucer knew Merton, or New College, or smaller Oxford halls with wardens (Albon Hall and Canterbury Hall had wardens about this date) he would see that the term was acceptable in both universities, while allowing him again to cover his tracks, or his barbs.

When the scholars realize that they have been duped, John says 'men wil us foles calle, Bathe the wardeyn and oure felawes alle' (4111–12). The manuscript variants for *oure* (*hise*, *oþir*) suggest that in this line (as distinct from 4203) at least two scribes may have read 'felawes' in the academic sense of *socii*, not simply as 'companions'. The *O.E.D.*'s first instance of this academic use is from Peacock's *Repressor* (*c.* 1449): 'that the maister and the felawis kepe the statutis of the collegis . . .'; but Peacock had been fellow of Oriel himself in 1415, and is doubtless using the vernacular terms current in his youth. *Socii* at this date covered all members on the foundation and is a mere synonym for *scolares*. In practice, however, the members

---

[1] A case brought against an early warden of Merton failed on the ground that in a Cambridge attorney's brief the term *magister* was used instead of *custos*: OHS N.S. xviii. 170. For the term *magister custos* in a case about Warden Wantyng's horse see *Curia Regis Rolls Ed. II*, ed. J. P. Collas (Selden Soc., 1965), p. 128.

of such a foundation cannot ever have had entirely equal status. Our two scapegraces may be technically *scolares* or *socii* (one lateish manuscript actually reads *felawes* for 'clerkes' at the beginning of the tale (4002)), but in fact must be, as we would say, undergraduates, subject to the warden and the discipline of the college: they have to beg permission of their warden to go as far as Trumpington (4008). They need not have been more than fourteen on entry. The striking point here is that King's Hall appears to have been the first English college to possess a sizeable undergraduate element which at the same time formed an integral part of the collegiate institution, and by 1350 this element shared 'a life in common with senior graduate members'; which is wholly consistent with inferences we might draw from the tale. Whatever the precise colour of 'felawes' in Chaucer's time, the word has never been used more aptly. The difference in status between clerks such as these and clerks such as the Oxford Nicholas, of the Miller's Tale, living 'allone withouten any companye', would strike any visitor or migrant from Oxford before the turn of the century, by which time New College there was accepting undergraduate members (though not under fifteen). But they are all alike *clerici*: clerks. The letters confirming the foundation of King's Hall in 1343 call it a *collegium clericorum*. It was because of this status that the statutes of 1380 forbade them to carry knife or dagger (*nullus . . . basilardum portet seu aliquem alium cultellum statui clericorum indecentem*). Yet the reeve is not inaccurate, nor are the clerks infringing the statutes when they set out 'with good swerd and with bokeler by hir syde' (4019): clerks were always allowed to carry weapons when travelling—hence the *arma* of the fellows of Merton.[1]

iii. Several manuscripts make our clerks not only young but 'poure' (4002)—which the metre permits if it does not

[1] See p. 8.

require. Nothing better illustrates the formulaic character of the phrase 'poor clerk' than its appearance here; instead of one 'poor scholar' in an Oxford house, the reeve gives us two in a Cambridge hall. But their poverty adds little more to the tale than Nicholas's did. They are called poor simply because scholars without exhibitions or benefices were assumed to be so. In the cognate French tales we find 'deus clers', 'deux povre clers', almost at random.[1]

If our clerks did indeed belong to the King's Hall, though they may have been *impecuniosi*, they were in no sense *impotentes*—the term used for scholars in dire need. All scholars of the Hall received $\frac{1}{2}d$. a week direct from the royal exchequer—at least enough to keep body and soul together, even if they had to supplement it from other sources. Dr. Cobban believes that the standard of living in the Hall was higher than in the rest of Cambridge. Nothing in the records suggests that the Hall recognized any category of 'poor scholars', rather the contrary: most of its members must have been reasonably well off. But socially their origins seem to have been varied. Often they were nominated at the instance of a court official or high-born patron: we find a son of a Master Smith in the Tower, or of the King's Cook or Serjeant-at-Arms alongside the cousin of the Bishop of Llandaff. Any scholar so nominated was likely to get some supplementary support from his patron—or, like Nicholas at Oxford—from 'friends'. In short, 'poor' is not integral to the conception of a King's Hall man, though it would be rash to assume that this is why some manuscripts omit it.

Chaucer makes it plain that John and Aleyn come from the north of the Trent; and northerners were not hard to find in fourteenth-century Cambridge: Peterhouse has strong northern connections. But no college at this time drew so many members from the North as King's Hall did. Between 1317 and 1443 the largest proportion of its

[1] See Appendix A.

scholars came from the Reeve's county of Norfolk, but Yorkshire stood almost as high—though there were very few from more northerly counties. Dr. Cobban argues that this may reflect the strong connection of the cathedral chapter of York with the central government. Dr. Highfield notes that Cambridge was easily accessible from York, which grew in importance during the Scottish wars. There may also have been a deliberate Cambridge move to attract or counterbalance the northern element that had been drawn to Oxford by Queen's College, which made special provision from its beginnings for Cumberland and Westmorland, as St. John's at Cambridge was to do later. To introduce northern scholars was itself to heighten the university interest of the tale, for the antagonism between North and South at both universities was notorious: the stipulation that fellows of Merton should refrain from regional scurrilities is but one example of its consequences.

But what did Chaucer mean by *'fer* in the north' (4015)? This is a question that only a philologist can answer. And a brilliant philologist and story-teller has answered it. Buried deep in the *Transactions of the Philological Society* for 1934 lies one of the first papers that the author of *The Lord of the Rings* ever published. If admirers of that work, or admirers of Chaucer, would study this paper they would learn something that no critics of either can teach. The pity is that since 1934 linguistics has elbowed philology out of the way and no one has bothered to test or extend Tolkien's findings on 'Chaucer as a philologist' in the light of new collations of the manuscripts or later place-name studies.[1] I shall take these findings largely, though not entirely, on trust; merely noting that Tyrwhitt tentatively anticipated some of them.

The matter would be simpler if we could identify the

---

[1] In MS. Paris Anglais 39 the dialect is 'levelled to North Midland' (Manly and Rickert, *The Text of the Canterbury Tales* (1940), i. 402, 405). C.U.L. MS. Gg iv 27 reduces the dialectal colouring, BO¹ increases it (ibid. i. 60).

'toun' (i.e. the village) 'that hiȝte Strother'. But it is precisely because it is a village that this is difficult. All one can say is that this name, both as a simplex and as an element, is now found only north of the Tees, in Durham and Northumberland—further north, that is, than Yorkshire. But 'Lange Strothere' is recorded in the North Riding in the thirteenth century, so 'strother' (meaning 'a place overgrown with brushwood') may have been more widely distributed then than now. John's oath 'by seint Cutberd' (4127)—regarded by Tolkien as a rustic malapropism (answering to the carpenter's 'Nowelis flood' in the Miller's Tale?) but probably a current form—certainly points to Durham or Northumberland, the *patrimonium Sancti Cutberti*, though this saint's feast had been commemorated nationally from early times. It was celebrated at the two Oxford colleges with northern associations— University and Queen's—and also by the monks at Durham Hall in Oxford. It still figures in the Oxford university almanac.[1] So Oxford readers would certainly take the point, even if to others the saint's name in this form conveyed no more than a vague outlandish suggestion.

In fact every word, every phoneme in the dialogue between the miller and the clerks was deliberately chosen to provoke a response in readers or listeners who would be chiefly southerners. The impact of the dialect would be far stronger then than now, when some northernisms, then distinctive, have become standard speech—like the pl. *-es* for southern *-eth* in 'How fares thy faire daughter and thy wyf?' (4023) or the pronoun *thair* in 4172, or Aleyn's very first words: 'Al hayl' (4022). As with the Reeve, not a moment is lost in establishing the northernness. And the

---

[1] The form 'Cutberd' is found in a Godstow document, and the saint's feast appears in both Godstow and Oseney calendars. University College still has a fine twelfth-century illuminated life of the saint, and a vellum fragment of a magnificent folio calendar in which his feast is marked as *duplex principale*. For celebrations at Durham Hall see OHS lx. 242.

sparse but precious evidence in the Reeve's own speech shows how nice was Chaucer's sense of local language. That northern pronoun *ik* used twice in his Prologue but nowhere else in the whole canon is reinforced at the conclusion of his tale by the distinctive Danelaw form *greythen* (4309: ON *greiða*); whilst *chymbe* ('the streem of lyf now droppeth on the chymbe', 3895) is a rare variant of *chime*, the later East Anglian term for the rim of a cask. Few though these forms are, they are sufficient to establish this North Norfolk narrator as the proper vehicle for northern dialogue at a time when East Anglia shared a great number of northern forms and words, and when King's Lynn was a centre of seaborne trade with the North. A Bawdswell man visiting Cambridge would be less puzzled or put off by the sounds that Trevisa described as 'scharp, frotinge and unschape' than a man of Kent or London.

Again, of the miller's talk, Chaucer gives no more than twenty lines. But at least one phrase smacks of a market town. 'False harlot', he calls John (4268). In Cambridge market, on a Saturday morning in 1294, one William Saxon complained that Margaret Paternoster called him 'harlot, gadeling, and scalled thief!' to the detriment of his business.[1] Two of these three terms are not found so early in the dictionaries. But nowhere else do we find 'a tare' used as the miller uses it (4056): it is just the image that would occur to a miller, accustomed to find vetch seeds in corn.

A question of John's epitomizes the linguistic comedy. When he finds that the horse has galloped off, he asks: 'Why nadstow pit the capul in the lathe?' (4088). *Pit* as a past tense is in Middle as in Modern English largely northern; *capul* ('horse') had spread through or from the north via alliterative verse, but is recorded in East Anglian colloquial use (in the *Promptorium Parvulorum*); and *lathe* an Old Norse word, still a northern term for 'barn', is

---

[1] *Cambridge Borough Documents*, ed. W. M. Palmer (1931), p. 9; cf. p. xiii.

found in the East Anglian *Genesis and Exodus*—but also (interestingly enough) in Chaucer's *Hous of Fame*, in an image associating him with reeves' and millers' concerns:

> For al mot out, other late or rathe,
> Alle the sheves in the lathe.   (2139–40)

How closely philological sensibility bears on our reading of the tale a final instance may show. Says John to Simkin:

> 'Oure manciple, I hope he wil be deed,
> Swa werkes ay the wanges in his heed'   (4029–30)

where 'hope' (in the sense of 'expect') is one sort of linguistic joke, 'swa' and the plural 'werkes' (= 'ache')—northernisms—are another, 'ay' a third; but 'wanges'—what are they? 'Back teeth' say the glosses, 'temples' says Tolkien, envisaging a feverish headache, and assuming Chaucer's adoption of the term from literary sources. That Chaucer relied on literary sources for his dialectal uses I venture to doubt; and that the manciple's malady was toothache—no light affliction in the Middle Ages—is suggested by a dialogue in a fifteenth-century Oxford schoolbook: 'It were better to eny of us all to be *dede*', says the boy-speaker, 'than to suffre such thynge as the maister hath sufferyde these thre dais agone in the tothe-ache.'[1]

iv. Turn we now (as the romances say) from the manciple's 'wanges' to the manciple himself. *Manciple* is the proper term for the officer who purchases provisions and such, for a college. But was it used, at this date, in the King's Hall, or anywhere in Cambridge? In the earliest King's Hall accounts the term *manicipulus* does occur, but by the 1360s it gives way in the records (though not necessarily in everyday use) to *pincerna*, 'butler'. But I cannot find that at King's Hall or anywhere else the butler

---

[1] *A Fifteenth-Century Schoolbook*, ed. W. A. Nelson (1956), p. 29.

H

managed the wheat or malt supply, or took it to be ground
(a task which is implied in our tale). At King's Hall the
administration was largely in the hands of a committee of
six 'seneschals', usually fellows with higher degrees in law.
But—and this is possibly pertinent—round about the
1380s, owing to a large number of deaths or resignations,
the running of the college fell upon young and inexperi-
enced scholars, not yet B.A.s, so that it was described as
'désolée et destitute de bone gouvernance'.[1] At any time
a college officer, be he bursar, seneschal, or manciple,
would find it advisable to keep an eye on the college miller,
as the reeve suggests (3995 ff.).

Is the term 'manciple' another piece of Oxbridge obfuscation? At Oxford manciples were part of the system from
the beginning, providing the commons: members of a hall
or college depended on him, and he on them, to the extent
that they contributed three pence a term towards his
stipend; and he sometimes joined, as Emden puts it, 'in
the mischievous exploits of the more boisterous members'.
One August night in 1389 three of them, using 'choppe-
chery' as their cry, ran amuck in Oxford, robbing and
beating up another manciple. Though at Cambridge
Pembroke (and later Corpus and Christ's) had manciples,
almost all references to the office occur in Oxford records.
A poem of 1401 has the line: 'oones I was a manciple at
Mertoun Halle',[2] and Merton certainly had a manciple up
to a century ago: one of them (previously butler) gave his
name to 'Patey's Quad', now destroyed. Queen's, New
College, Canterbury Hall, 'Albon' Hall likewise had the
office, as All Souls still does.

Chaucer's other manciple, 'wise in byyinge of vitaille',
is 'of a temple' (*CT* A 567–9)—that is, of the Middle or
Inner Temple. Interestingly enough, he is credited with

[1] Cf. Cobban, op. cit., p. 171.
[2] *Political Poems* (ed. T. Wright), ii. 98. There was a tenement called 'Manciples' next to Magdalen Hall: OHS lxvi. 147.

deploying—as the miller does—a 'lewed mannes wit' against the academic wisdom of legists (574–5). And I here interpolate the conjecture that the two clerks of our tale were themselves reading law. If they were at the King's Hall the likelihood of this is great: about half the entire stock of its library was composed of books of civil law—appropriate reading enough for future civil servants —and there were four times as many on canon law as on theology. The last recorded bequest of Edward III was a gift of five civil-law texts—made through William of Wykeham, as chancellor of the realm, in 1368, for the special benefit of Walter de Herford, K.S. The contrast with the Merton library is striking. In Cambridge, Trinity Hall, later to become the most notable legal college, had at this time only 'the basic civil law texts'; Corpus, founded in 1356, had only eighteen such texts. The earliest catalogue of King's College, a fifteenth-century foundation (distinct from King's Hall), lists not a single civil-law text out of its 175 manuscripts. King's Hall, moreover, provided a fifth or more of the total number of legists in the university at this period and most of its graduates who took second degrees were civil or canon lawyers.

It is not surprising, then, if John is a Kingsman, that he thinks of the loss of his corn in legal terms, citing a legal maxim (4179 ff.) of which the Harleian manuscript supplies the Latin form: 'qui in uno gravatur, in alio debet relevari' ('if a man in a poynt be ygreved, in another he sal be releved'). He speaks also of 'amendement' and 'esement' (4185–6), both terms with a legal flavour, even if that flavour is not obvious here; indeed the precise sense of 'compensation' here required is evidenced only once again, in a legal contract of later date.

v. Fifthly and finally we are told that the scholars had 'hir whete and eek hir malt' ground at Trumpington Mill (3991).

A mill figures in the French analogues to the tale, but with no mention of malt. The line leads us to the very basis of college life. In any college accounts for the period, but notably in those of King's Hall, wheat and the barley (*brasium*) from which malt was made, hold the main place. Since ale was a main item of sustenance (far more was spent on it than on bread) malt was naturally mentioned along with wheat. East Anglian malt was renowned, and an article of export. The provision of both was a bursar's principal care. At Cambridge he could expect to buy his cereals in the city market, or at Fen Ditton, a mile up the Cam, whence they could be brought down by river and landed at Cornhithe, very close to King's Hall. But as new colleges meant more mouths to feed the pressure on supplies must have increased; and it was to ease it that King's *College* in 1452 was to buy the manor of Grantchester from the Burghershes (to whom Thomas Chaucer had been related by marriage). It lies next to Trumpington within easy reach of the college, so that the manor-harvest could supply grain for college bakery and manor house, the corn being ground at Grantchester mill. Even so, the King's College bursars often had to buy wheat a bushel at a time on the Cambridge market.

King's Hall likewise had a bakery, a granary (as did Merton), and a sizeable brew-house, but not a malt-house (which King's College had later at Grantchester). The soil and harvests being generally good in the Cambridge area, the scholars, and even the servants, of King's Hall, ate wheaten bread, not the barley bread of the peasant classes.[1]

---

[1] So barley could be kept for malting. In the fifteenth century the manor of King's College at Grantchester produced more malt than wheat (beer was given to occasional labourers there instead of commons).

The entrance fee to the Cambridge Guild of St. Mary was two quarters of malt, its stores of grain and malt being sold to members at fixed prices. Malt was a common medium of exchange: hence the limitour in the Summoner's Tale begs for 'a busshel whete, malt or reye / A goddes kechyl or a trype of chese' (D 1746–7).

Their malt they probably purchased on the open market. The guild of St. Mary at Cambridge derived much of its income from malt which it sold, with wheat, to its members at fixed prices. It also did a good business in millstones—an indispensable item in this kind of economy, which literally pivoted on the mill.[1] The Cambridge Corpus Christi guild included at least two millers (one called Harry Scott).

Certainly, then, there were mills in Cambridge. Three are mentioned in Domesday Book: the King's and Bishop's Mills on the main stream of the Cam, and Newnham Mill on the branch. Mill buildings were a feature of the town up to Gwen Raverat's time, as readers of her *Period Piece* will remember; they will remember too a house called the Hermitage, successor to a real hermitage where lived the hermit whose pious duty it was to keep the bridge that led to the mills in repair.

Why then should the clerks carry their wheat as far as Trumpington, three miles away? For the same reasons that later led King's College to farm Grantchester manor and rent Grantchester Mill. The growth of colleges, not to mention the earlier establishments of the friars, must have severely taxed the milling resources of the city, dependent as they were on a small and sluggish river: Camus, as Milton so rightly remarked, comes 'footing slow'. In any case the building of a fulling-mill in 1353 had still further diminished the flow of water; the King's Mill and Newnham Mill could not work at the same time: the King's miller blew a horn to warn the Newnham miller to stop grinding. The contrast with Oxford, with its abundance of streams serving at least seventeen mills, is striking. As late as the seventeenth century when the city of Cambridge tried to monopolize the Town Mill, the University protested that 'it will not seeme meete or reasonable to have the foode of breade for two thousand

[1] *CAS* xxxix. xvi; Willis and Clark, op. cit. ii. 398.

students . . . depende uppon the service of one mill, not beinge able to turne into meale the fifthe parte of the graine that is there sente . . .'[1] In Chaucer's day the new colleges had no claim on the services of the local mills, and they were too near to them to get sufficient head of water for mills of their own, which would moreover have impeded river traffic; Trumpington was the nearest alternative, and accessible from the London highway.

So to Trumpington the clerks go, taking the warden's palfrey, Bayard (4073–5), from the college stables. The head of a house was allowed to keep a horse at its expense, but no scholar was permitted to keep even a hack. At Oxford the warden of Merton likewise rode a palfrey, and we know the names of some of his horses.[2] The grooming of horses also figures in the records: Merton evidently had a full-time groom (*palefredarius*, or *sumetarius*) with 'the vital job of keeping the warden's horses in trim'. John and Aleyn would be in for a slating when they took Bayard back in a filthy state: this is part of the 'hething', the contumely that they fear (4110).

A single sack of wheat would be as much as their steed could carry, and probably not much more than they had in the granary, since colleges evidently bought by the quarter or the bushel—flour might grow mouldy if stored. Sword and buckler seem hardly necessary. But amongst the pilgrims the Miller is so armed, and the Reeve himself carries a rusty blade. Where there ran a highway, robbers might also run; and clerks took up *gladii et boclearii et cultelli* on any excuse.

They would go through the Trumpington gate, across a bridge over the King's Ditch; one reason they have later

---

[1] BM Cole MS. 5882, cit. *CAS* xiv. 231.

[2] See OHS N.S. xviii, *passim*. These Merton accounts regularly show expenses for horses, e.g. 'in pastronibus' ('hobbles': if Aleyn and John had had pasterns their 'capul' would not have run off so easily), 'boucles ad surcengle', a cord 'vocatum rerecorde', 'a black pottle of fat to smear on Sakedras and Barhude', etc.

to crave lodging for the night is that the town gates would
be closed at dark; no one travelled after sunset. And they
would pass the House or Hall of St. Peter on the right and
a little further on the left, the Spital house of St. Antony
and St. Éloi (whom the Prioress swore by): it had been
built about 1360, on 'the toune ende' where hospitals and
leper houses always stood. The village of Trumpington
was just beginning to spread out along the London road—
the road a Norfolk reeve would take coming to Cambridge
via Fowlmere, or from Shelford or Chesterford. It probably
had no inn, only an ale-house or two; which would explain
why the clerks could not expect to find beds there—and
also why the miller can send Malin off to buy ale. Essentially the kind of man who would be free with other
people's money, he seizes on their offer of silver for
provender, to obtain the best and strongest local ale
(famed in Thackeray's time, and perhaps in Chaucer's),
most of which he dispatches himself (4149, 4162). The
other houses clustered round the church—the parish being
of just the opposite kind from that to which Chaucer's
village parson ministered: 'Wyd was *his* parisshe, and
houses fer asonder' (which suggests High Suffolk rather
than the Fens). Chaucer speaks properly of the 'parson of
the town' (3943) because, though sometimes no better
than he should be, the rector of Trumpington *was* a parson, enjoying full possession of the dues of the benefice
and the rights of pasture that sometimes brought parsons
into conflict with reeves. We know the names of some of
Trumpington's fourteenth-century parsons. One of them,
Ricardus dictus Berde de Ledbury, was in 1343 succeeded
by Richard, his son: as scandalous a circumstance as that
which led to the miller's alliance (3943): the suggestion
that the parson's daughter is 'of noble kin' is clearly
satirical; and we should not be surprised that she enjoys
the later 'swiving' (4230). The real parson's behaviour
may indeed have been *too* scandalous. Immediately after

Richard junior had been instituted, the church was applied to the prioress and convent of Haliwell, who evidently ejected him forthwith. In that convent, or at St. Radegunde's in Cambridge, a Trumpington miller's wife might well have been brought up—'she was yfostred in a nonnerye' (3946).[1] Whether or not Chaucer knew the local situation every line here, in Hardy's phrase, is 'done from the real'. A similar situation of son succeeding father as rector is found at Grantchester, just across the river.

Chaucer may never have come to Trumpington but he knew Sir Roger of that name, whose tomb may still be seen in the fine village church, for the two men held positions in the Royal Household at the same time: Sir Roger being responsible for the payment of the last of Edward III's annuities to Chaucer's wife Philippa, of the same household. By 1379 Chaucer and his wife had a place on John of Gaunt's payroll and Roger had obtained a place in the duke's household for his wife Blanche, and we find the duke giving New Year gifts to 'dame Blanche de Trumpington, et Phelippe Chaucy'.[2] Chaucer would know that at least two people of his acquaintance might scrutinize his Reeve's Tale carefully. Yet another member of the Royal household in Philippa's time was Lady Ferrars. *Her* husband possessed the fee of Trumpington manor; a Robert Ferrars had been an esquire in the king's household in Chaucer's time (1369), and was in 1386 admitted to the fraternity of Lincoln cathedral at the same time as Philippa Chaucer. Still another member of the royal household

---

[1] For a parson's daughter see *Paston Letters and Papers*, ed. N. Davis (1971), p. 227. Cf. *Speculum*, xliv (1970), 202, and Wiclif, *English Works*, ed. Arnold, iii. 190. The bowdlerizing scribe of MS. Harl. 733 makes her a swanherd's daughter brought up in a dairy. For a rector's daughter living in a nunnery see *Testamenta Eboracensia*, i. 18.

[2] *Chaucer Life Records* (1966), p. 90. But the editors of the *Records* have unfortunately omitted the part of the entry in John of Gaunt's Register for 6 March 1381 which also mentions Dame Blanche, who is again mentioned along with Philippa Chaucer in a similar entry for 6 May 1382.

contemporary with Chaucer was Thomas, earl of Oxford:
the earls of Oxford held land in Grantchester.

The church and village of Trumpington were large
enough to have a guild, the guild of St. Mary. It would
turn out in force on those holidays on which the miller's
wife showed off her 'gyte of reed' (3954); and she expected
that 'a lady sholde hir spare' (3966)—that a Dame Blanche
would recognize her as near-equal!

Between Trumpington church and the river Cam lay
fields of arable edged by river meadows. The wheat grown
would be ground at Trumpington mill, which lay just beyond a copse, still marked by a stand of beech—a piece of
woodland deliberately preserved or renewed to provide
wood for firing and mast and 'swych panage' for swine.
Through this copse today two tracks lead to a pool on the
river, and at least one of them may be ancient.

Now at this point the river ceases to be called the Rhee,
and becomes the Cam. It is something more than a brook,
the term used by the Reeve (3922); though at this point
too it is joined by the Bourn, which has always been called
a brook. To be within the Trumpington boundaries the
mill should lie on the main stream (though for some
unexplained reason one or two acres across the stream
have always been in Trumpington parish, not Grantchester). A century ago a local historian said that the
foundations of a mill could still be seen under the water
at the spot now called Byron's pool. It requires the eye of
faith to see them now; but before Byron's time the place
was known as the Old Mills, suggesting that it was a
double mill like several at Oxford and like those further
down the river at Cambridge. In that case the miller would
use one set of stones for wheat, the other for malt or
barley. The mill-pool would provide the fish that Simkin
the miller was so skilled in catching (3927)—and eels,
taken by the thousand in this area; the fishing and riparian
rights pertaining to a mill, as a reeve would know, were

almost as important as the mill itself.[1] The bridge mentioned at the beginning of the tale (3922), perhaps higher
up than the present bridge (built 1790), would bring the
scholars across the stream (a picture in Fitzwilliam MS.
165 shows just such a scene) to unload their wheat. A sack
normally held up to four bushels, medieval measure, which
was about a fifth less than ours; the Ellesmere artist gives
Robin the Miller of the Prologue a symbolic sack, as well
as the pipes alluded to at 3927. Only the miller would
know how much flour it should make, so he can extract his
half bushel with impunity. And the clerks must speak him
fair, as he has no obligation to grind for them. The college
did not own the mill. Normally, doubtless, the manciple would take a sack of corn every week or so, collecting
the flour milled from the grain left on the previous visit—
a routine that would give no occasion to supervise the
grinding.

To judge from medieval representations of East Anglian mills, our mill would be of the overshot type used for
a shallow head of water, with wooden wheels about nine
inches wide. It would probably be a one-storeyed affair,
with a projecting loft—known in local dialect as a lew-
come. Adjoining the mill proper there would be a two- or
three-roomed house. One room is a kitchen or parlour,
another a chamber where the whole family sleeps: the
bedding would be of sedge cut on the near-by fen, known
locally as 'fen down'; just what the clerks would sleep on
in college; it was landed at Sedgys hall, opposite Magdalene. The 'chamber is dark', even by moonlight, which
enters only through a hole (4217, 4298); so it may be in

---

[1] Hence banks, weirs, and sluices were the subject of constant lawsuits and
remained so until George Eliot's time. Cf. OHS xc. 461 ff., 470 f., 477 f., and
Oxford City Records, p. 177 (1545). Tithes were payable on fish taken in the mill
dam (*CAS* xiv. 186), and the tithes of a mill might be paid in fish: *Godstow Register*
(EETS o.s. 129), p. 322. For leasing of fishing pertaining to a mill see *BPR* iv.
434. For specific mention of mill waters and fish-traps therein see OHS ci. 71,
and for receipts from a mill-weir ibid. 196.

a loft. Behind the mill is a barn (or lathe 4088) where
wheat malt or barley would be kept, and a *levesel* (4061)
—a term of courtly poetry that we hardly expect to find
in this context: it seems to mean a rustic shelter, possibly
a frame or lean-to of poles thatched with reeds bound down
with sedge covering the back door or steps of the mill.[1]
Since it is behind the mill, it would face south to the
stretch of open country that is still, though drained and
cultivated, called Lingay Fen. As Bayard is eventually
caught in a ditch, some primitive draining had perhaps
begun. The river was not then embanked, but flooded
constantly, and made its way into its own channels. The
names of White Ditch Field, Crown Ditch furlong, and
Little Fen, on a seventeenth-century field map of near-by
Grantchester testify to such a configuration. There is some
evidence for a ford across the Bourn to Lingay Fen, and
if there was no bridge the clerks would be wet-footed
before they began their chase.

It is for this fen (as Skeat suggested) that Bayard makes
as soon as the miller unties him. There were wild mares,
and there was the rich unfenced pasture. 'Wild' does not
necessarily mean 'untamed' or ownerless. The mares may
be merely youthful and frisky, having been put out for
what grazing there was after hay-harvest. A Grantchester
field near by was called Horsecroft, perhaps because it was
used for the same purpose. To gain some notion of the
fourteenth-century scene—so different from today's placid
fields—we should go across to Fulbourn Fen or further out
to Wicken Fen, 700 acres of damp grassland, undrained
and unploughed, where even now a high water-level often
makes the cutting of the sedge-crop difficult; Woodwal-
ton Fen (Hunts.) perhaps gives a still better picture of

---

[1] Cf. *he(ve)d selle*, 'canopy or covering over the hoist of a mill', 1412: *A
Medieval Farming Glossary*, ed. J. L. Fisher (1968). A mill still working at
Hingham, Cornwall, has a lean-to over the platform at the rear of the mill where
grain is unloaded.

'the primal scene as it were'; to walk there is indeed to go 'thurgh thikke and thurgh thenne' (4066). But 'by the way' (4114) may suggest that they found a track going back to the mill: 'the way' was a local term for such tracks: compare Derham Way, Millway, in Grantchester Hundred.

There is some indication that before the draining of the Fens horses abounded in the wilds of Cambridgeshire. Horseheath, some ten miles to the south, was probably what its name implies. Long before Newmarket became famous for horse-racing there was a horse fair at Exning, near by. Stourbridge horse-fair near Cambridge was equally famous, and lasted till 1935. Up till the Second World War gypsies came to the Fens to pasture their horses and breed their foals on the common land.

The miller knows that Bayard will make for the mares; and its 'we hee' proves him right. It is the whinny of sexual desire. In the morality play the *Trial of Treasure* (1567) Inclination, led in by the bridle, says: 'Wee he-he-he-he. Ware the horse heels. I would the reins were loose, that I might run away.' 'Such hahees, teehees wild colts play', says Lily. And Langland transfers the whinny to lustful men (*Piers Plowman* B vii. 91). So it has its place in a tale where the horses' masters, and even the village parson, act out their sexual urges.

Meanwhile the miller has done what the jolly miller of nursery rhyme does—as often, a children's game preserves a gay version of an originally harsh reality:

> As the wheel went round he made his pelf:
> One hand in the hopper, and the other in the bag,
> As the wheel went round he made his grab,

that is, he made his pelf, his illicit profit, both by taking handfuls of corn fed into the hopper, on one floor, and by stealing flour as it flows into the bag below. That is why two observers would be necessary to outwit him. And they could plausibly profess an interest in the mechanism

(4039 ff.). The machinery of the mill must have had a rare fascination in days when there was hardly any other. It kept it for Maggie Tulliver, who 'loved the resolute din, the unresting motion of the great stones, the sweet pure scent of the meal'. It keeps it today, as one watches the grain gently pouring down from the hopper into the wooden shoe above the millstone and thence into the 'eye' of the runner-stone (the *oculus petrae* of medieval terminology) which all the while makes its 'low rumble'.

At the end of the story the clerks go back with their flour, and a 'cake' into the bargain—i.e. a flat loaf of bread like one the Summoner took to Canterbury. Trumpington is to Cambridge as Oseney is to Oxford: it is a comparison that would occur to the Norfolk Reeve as he listened to the Miller's Oxford story. But the 'play' at Trumpington —'play' is a key word in both tales—has been cruder and the participants coarser. As against Alison, pretty as pear-tree in spring and jolly as a young colt, the wench Malin is broad-buttocked, camus-nosed; Alison sings like a swallow, Malin's mother chatters like a jay. The pejorative comparisons implied are part of the Reeve's character. But they are also part of the character of Cambridge. Oxford, if poets can be trusted, has always had the wittiest men, and the prettiest girls, beginning with the blonde who is the heroine of the Anglo-French romance *Jehan et Blonde*: whereas—if poets can be trusted—Malin was a Cambridge prototype:

> Here I live [sighed Thomas Randolph] in Cambridge air
> Where truth to tell there's few be fair,
> And none to kiss, save, now and then,
> The sunburnt faces of the fen.

And so Rupert Brooke of Grantchester:

> Ditton girls are mean and dirty
> And there's none at Harston under thirty.

Cambridge clerks have not always been uncouth swains, though the bucks of Gray's time frightenened him by setting women on their heads in the street, but they have continued—witness Pendennis, F. W. Maitland, and the *alumni* of Trinity Hall—to show a penchant for the law.

By some uncanny instinct Chaucer has adumbrated in these two tales features that were to grow more, not less, distinctive as the centuries passed. 'Hende' Nicholas's cleverness was to become the urbane sophistication of a Wilde, the wit of our latter-day Mercurius Oxoniensis. Oxford has remained a tradesman's city, Cambridge a market town. The very tightness with which the two tales are bound together emphasizes the contrast.

I have tried to show that the Reeve knew what he was talking about: which is to say that Chaucer did. The poet whose favourite metaphors for the making of poetry were drawn from field and barn and furrow must have watched with a special attentiveness the life of the mill. A capital at Vézelay shows Saint Paul grinding the wheat of the Old Law to make the bread of the New. In these tales Chaucer is grinding the rough grain of fabliau into the fine flour of local character and local story. The fabliau that went its own way issued in such ballads as the Cuckolded Miller— which ought by rights to be printed as an analogue to the Reeve's Tale.[1] But the wheels of fiction that his tale sets in motion will turn to different effect. Simkin will give place to a miller and maltster called Tulliver (who yet talks the Reeve's language: 'Wakem knows meal from bran; the gray colt may chance to kick like his black sire'). And in the fullness of time the mill on the Cam will give place to the Mill on the Floss.

[1] *The Oxford Book of Ballads,* ed. J. Kinsley, no. 138.

APPENDIX A

Poor Scholars

THE terms 'poor scholar'[1] or 'poor clerk' occur repeatedly in university documents, as the index to Lynn Thorndike's *University Records and Life in the Middle Ages* (1944) will show: e.g. one of the oldest colleges in Paris was 'the hostel of the poor scholars of St. Nicholas of the Louvre' (op. cit., p. 31); the earliest Statutes of the Sorbonne speak of fragments of food put in 'a common repository for poor clerks' (p. 89). Papal documents also refer to this category of scholar: e.g. Clement VI offered benefices to all poor clerks who came to the papal court in the first months of his pontificate (see R. W. Southern, *Western Society and the Church in the Middle Ages* (1970), p. 161); and the Third Lateran Council referred to benefices that would enable a master to give free tuition to poor scholars (Brian Tierney, *The Medieval Poor Law* (1959), p. 19). But the degree of poverty envisaged is rarely indicated. E. F. Jacob's essay in the *Bulletin of the John Rylands Library*, xxix (1946), though providing much material of interest, hardly answers the questions it raises, and A. Lloyd, in *The Early History of Christ's College* (p. 356), similarly skirts the issue. Rashdall states that by 'poor scholar' college founders meant only a scholar unable to support himself without assistance, and notes that in some statutes there is a fixed limit of income.[2] The

[1] The Oxford distinction between scholars and commoners first appears in the Statutes of St. John's (1560). At King's Hall, Cambridge, a distinction was made in the fourteenth century between *clerici pauperes* and *scolares qui sufficientem habent exhibitionem ad universitatem* (Cobban, *The King's Hall*, p. 77).

[2] H. Rashdall, *The Universities of Europe in the Middle Ages* (rev. Powicke and Emden, 1936), ii. 405 n. 1. At Oxford 'batellers' waited on other students before sitting down themselves (ibid.).

From the terms of a York will (that of Wm. Haytor, 1435) it appears that £5 p.a. was regarded as sufficient to keep a scholar at Oxford. Haytor left most of his estate 'ad exhibendum pro termino octo annorum in universitate Oxoniensi pauperes capellanos qui, antequam ad exhibicionem per executores meos admittantur, sint in artibus baccalarii, ad gradum ulteriorem in eisdem ingressuri; recipiatque eorum quilibet similiter annis termini antedicti centum solidos ad suam annualem pensionem' (*Testamenta Eboracensia*, ii. 57–8).

For the expenses of a scholar at Cambridge in the late fourteenth century

dearth of provisions, as Jacob remarks, made for high prices, so most scholars might plead poverty. Once at least (in 1297) *pauperes scolares* seems to be equivalent to *all* scholars of Oxford (OHS lxxxv. 137).

Donors regularly made provision for a number of poor scholars, but money so left usually provided loans rather than gifts.[1] Balliol was founded expressly for 'elemosinam pauperum scholarium' (*Oxford Balliol Deeds*, ed. H. E. Salter (1913), p. 280).[2] The Merton Statutes laid down that 'duodecim scolares pauperes secundarii' were to get 6*d.* a week for saying prayers for the souls of Henry of Almain, and Richard King of the Romans, benefactors of the founder (OHS N.s. xviii. 72, 391).[3] Donors frequently made such conditions. Thus an Oxford citizen in 1382 left to poor scholars 10*s.* 'pro psalteriis dicendis pro salute anime mee' (OHS lxiv. 257). One Balliol scholar was to be given each day 'reliquias sue mense' (p. 279). But that a 'poor scholar' might have some means of his own is indicated by the injunction of Archbishop Kilwardby to Merton (1276) allowing those who received an allowance of 4*d.* a week to augment it by 2*d.* of their own (OHS N.s. xviii. 72).[4] A bishop of Coventry decreed that scholars who lack necessities may carry holy water *per villas rurales*, receiving in return offerings that would otherwise go to the parish clerk (Legg, Preface to his edition of *The Clerk's Book of 1549*; cf. p. 43 above). The clerks whom chancellors licensed to beg must have been very poor;[5] but it must be remembered that the friars had made begging respectable.

see M. R. James, *A Descriptive Catalogue of the Manuscripts in the Library of Peterhouse*, pp. 58, 62.

[1] Rashdall, ii. 411. For the condition of poverty as applying to *consanguinei* of a family see now G. D Squibb, *Founder's Kin* (1972), chapter 1 and pp. 165–6.

[2] A similar phrase is used in a letter to the Bishop of Chichester from the Chancellor of the University, *c.* 1307–10: OHS N.s. iv. 10 (note: '. . . ne [elemosina] pereat per cautelas machinancium subversionem').

[3] *Secundarii* evidently refers to 'clerks in the second form' (in choir)—known at Lincoln as 'poor clerks': F. W. Harrison, *Music in Medieval Britain* (1958), p. 6.

Henry III caused all the poor clerks of Oxford to be fed in his hall there on the day when exsequies were said for his mother's soul (Liberate Roll, 30 Hen. III, cit. T. Hudson Turner, *Domestic Architecture* . . . (1851), p. 211).

[4] For a 'placita coram rege de pensione cuidam pauperi scholari in subsidium assignata' (1405–6) see Bodl. MS. Rawl. C 426, f. 136.

[5] Cf. *CAS* xv. 133.

It must also be remembered that a degree course lasting sixteen or twenty years might well impoverish a candidate; and there are cases of graduands who apply for reduction of fees: e.g. Richard Thornden, O.S.B., who in 1527 supplicated for the reduction of the grace for his D.D. on the grounds that his church cannot give him a single penny because of royal exactions; he has lost the favour and goodwill of most of his friends while pursuing his studies, and been put to expenses that he might have avoided had he studied abroad. His fee was reduced to £2 on condition that he said two Masses for the good estate of the regent masters (OHS n.s. viii. 258).

At the very end of the fifteenth century Cardinal Morton left £128. 3s. 8d. per annum to pay for at least thirty poor scholars; two-thirds of these, including two monks of Christ Church Canterbury, were to go to Oxford, the remainder to Cambridge. The Oxford scholars were allotted to various colleges, and lists of payments for them for the years 1501–8 survive (OHS n.s. viii. 266 ff.).[1] On the very last page of these English displaces Latin, and the term 'exhibition' (= 'maintenance'; cf. p. 117 n. 1 above) appears for the first time. For fourteenth-century payments by Magdalen to 'two or three pore schollers borne in Lanchishire . . . of the college of Brasenose' see OHS lxviii. 465.

At Peterhouse, Cambridge (whose statutes were modelled on Merton's), need was a prerequisite for a scholar; and Henry VI laid it down that 'every student selected for our royal college at Cambridge must be a poor and indigent clerk who has received the first tonsure' (cit. E. Rickert, *Chaucer's World*, p. 129).

'Poor scholar' evidently still had a clearly understood meaning a century ago: in 1858 Dean Liddell wrote: 'Most poor scholars who could benefit from an academical education will find places on Foundations in some college or other' (cit. Bill and Mason, *Christ Church and Reform* (1970), p. 56).

---

[1] Oseney Abbey at the same time paid 26s. 8d. to the Proctors 'in perpetuam eleemosynam pauperum scolarium' (OHS ci. 247, 276, 261).

A gift which may have been unique in kind was that of Reginald de Bodel, who in 1294 left 'to the community of poor scholars' the house in which he lived —which evidently became absorbed in St. Mary Hall. The University maintained a Mass for the donor (OHS lxx. 302).

APPENDIX B

Mills and Milling

THERE is no adequate study of the place of the water-mill in the medieval English (or European) economy,[1] or even of its construction. The pre-Conquest mill found recently at Tamworth, Staffs., is probably the earliest structure of its kind to be excavated in north-west Europe (see *The Times*, 19 Aug. 1971). It was of vertical undershot type, with an iron bearing; some of the mill-stones were of Rhineland lava (millstones of later date imported from Bavaria have been found in Bishopsgate). The interior of a twelfth-century mill is shown in detail in a MS. of Herrade de Landberg (see Jean Gimpel, *The Cathedral Builders* (trans. 1961), p. 163). It shows the inverted pyramidal hopper that remained general: cf. L. C. Hunter in *Technology and Culture*, viii (1967), 447 ff.

Detailed specifications for the (re)building of certain mills were printed by L. F. Salzman, *Building in England down to 1540* (1952), App. B 41, 86 (see also 119). In the second of these contracts the corn-mill and malt-mill are distinguished: the whole work, except for the cogwheel and waterwheel of the corn-mill and the 'melesills',[2] is to be done in five weeks at the cost of £11. 13s. 4d. (1467); in the other contract (1387) Henry Yevele and others contract to build two mills at Southwark within nine months for £45, including new wheels and axles and boards for the pool.

For a detailed list of 'Costs of a mill' see Baker, *History of Northamptonshire* (1822–30), i. 279, 281.

One of the most detailed pictures of a medieval mill is found in the East Anglian Luttrell Psalter (*c.* 1340), f. 181; a one-story

---

[1] Such a study would be based on Marc Bloch's suggestive article (1935: trans. in *Land and Work in Medieval Europe*, 1968), which draws on some English sources.

[2] Possibly the 'forsille and taillsille' (i.e. the top and bottom horizontal beams of the sluice gates) specified in another contract, which includes the making of a new weir and 'tumblyng bayes' (chutes; a phrase still used in Oxford) to the said weir (Salzman, p. 578).

building of stone (?) blocks in a wooden frame, with an overshot wheel fed by a chute from a dammed-up river. In the mill pond are two basket-work traps for fish and eels: cf. the woodcut in C. Singer and E. J. Holmyard, *History of Technology* (1956), ii, Fig. 542. Of earlier date is that in MS. Bodl. 764 (f. 44) showing an undershot wheel set in a chute and the gearing transmitting the drive, the hopper, and the ground corn emerging from the housing of the stones: illustrated in *Bodleian Picture Book* 14 (n.d.), Pl. 26. Cf. also Douce 256, f. 183ᵛ; Douce 135, f. 98, shows a two-storey mill, and Bodl. 968, f. 150, a tall mill of five gables. Other manuscript examples will be found in the Bodleian card index of miniatures. A Suffolk mill, *temp.* Edward IV, in the east window of the north aisle of Thaxted church possibly represents the mill stream of Tilby Abbey near by: it shows a tiled roof: see *CAS* xv. 26, Pl. 3. The undershot system was suitable for a constant, fast current, the overshot for a variable or sluggish flow. The miller built up a head of water which was diverted through a chute to the wheel, set below the level of the supply channel.

The oldest mill extant is said to be Bourn Mill, Colchester. An admirable account of two mills that were operating on the river Deben twenty years ago (Wickham Market and Ash Mill) appeared in the *East Anglian Magazine* for March 1948, with a plan of the elaborate water-system. An overshot mill at Cotehele, Cornwall, has been restored by the National Trust.

The multitude of representations of the water-mill testify to its place in daily life. Almost invariably they include a man or woman, usually with a horse, bearing a sack of grain: see, e.g., MS. Bodl. 264, ff. 49 and 81, and bosses at Norwich and Wells. They illustrate the anonymous passage cit. *Paston Letters and Papers*, ed. N. Davis (1971), p. xli: Clement Paston 'rodd to mylle on the bar hors bak wyth hys corn under hym and brought hom mele ageyn under hym And had . . . a vj skore acrys of lond with a lytyll pore watyrmylle rennynge by a lytylle ryver'. The miller's wife would play the same sociable role in the regular visits to the mill as is described by George Bourn in *A Farmer's Life* (1922) 500 years later. She is seen in a miniature in MS. Bodl. 276, f. 130ᵛ, spinning at the mill door. Such visits made the mill a regular source of news, like the market (cf. *Ancrene Wisse*, EETS o.s. 249, p. 48). The casual allusions to the horse at the mill, and the frog sitting coolly 'under the cog', in *The*

Owl and the Nightingale 778, 86, and to dogs driving rats out of the mill in *Havelok* 1966–7 may also be noted. In the Towneley *Prima Pastorum* Slawpase brings a sack of meal 'fro the myln whele'. Malt and barley sacks customarily held four bushels (the medieval bushel being of slightly less weight than today's).[1]

A miller's duties are mentioned in Walter of Henley's *Husbandry* passim: see especially pp. 83–4 in D. Olschinsky's edition (1971). Some technical terms for the parts of a mill found in Essex records are glossed by J. L. Fisher in *A Medieval Farming Glossary* (1968): e.g. *bacula, billa, bolstre, braaz, fetherbord, flemdiche* (mill-race), *fusillus, melegrave* (wood near a mill), *mellecrow, paskes, stagnum, stertes, trendle, vythelbord*. For a spindle (*fusillus*) and a scoop (*scopa*) see OHS N.S. xviii. 205.

The early accounts of King's College (examined by J. Saltmarsh in *Economic History Review*, iii (1936), 155 ff.) show how a college obtained its cereals. By 1484 King's had its own baker and brewer and had bought the manor of Grantchester (429 acres); but its harvest was insufficient to supply the flour required: once the bursar had to buy 80 quarters from one John Lete, and often he had to buy a bushel at a time on the Cambridge market, 'painfully aggregating the tiny surpluses of country peasants'. At first the wheat must have been ground in the town, but in 1484 the college leased Grantchester Mill[2] (within easy reach) and then had the benefit of tolls deducted in corn from local users. It also had the tithe corn of the rectory of Fulbourn. Barley was used solely for malting and stock-feed. (For the later history of Grantchester mill see Appendix C.)

Similar accounts for Oxford colleges have yet to be studied. But it seems from the thirteenth-century Merton Rolls (OHS N.S. xviii) that Merton benefited from the moiety of Holywell mill given to the college by the abbot of Oseney *c.* 1270: the mill and the fishing pertaining to it figure on the accounts from 1277. At one time the abbot provided a horse for carrying sacks thither: OHS xc. 186–8 (cf. N.S. xviii. 205). A mill built by Magdalen College on the same branch of the Cherwell was pulled down in 1486 as constituting an

---

[1] For a striking 'similitude' between the activities of a mill and the human heart see *Memorials of Saint Anselm*, ed. R. W. Southern and F. S. Schmitt (1969), p. 53.

[2] The plural form 'mills' is used in the *Valor Ecclesiasticus* of Henry VIII (ii. 226).

impediment to the Holywell mill, and it was agreed that the course of the water at 'Yryschmannys Pole' was to be 'directed by sadde men of the contre' (OHS lxxvi. 87–8; cf. 321).

A good account of mills in and around Cambridge was compiled by H. P. Stokes: *CAS* xiv. 183–233. The following points should be noted:

i. Newnham Mill and the King's Mill were the only water-mills in Cambridge; the bishop of Ely's mill was alongside the King's Mill (they were under one roof by the sixteenth century), and presumably ground for the bishop. Both are shown as undershot in Braun's map, *c.* 1575.

ii. The manor of Newnham, including the (two-wheeled) mill, was transferred to Gonville Hall early in the sixteenth century; the college leased the manor to a miller but presumably had its own grain ground there (*Cambridge Borough Documents*, pp. 73, 93). Gonville later owned a mill at Shelford. Corpus bought a water-mill at Fen Ditton in Mathew Parker's time (see Nasmith, *Catalogus* (1786), p. 105).

iii. Some corn was brought up river by boat as far as the King's Mill till the nineteenth century. Millstones, being heavy, also came by boat: see *Cambridge Borough Documents*, p. 68, Willis and Clark, ii. 398. Soft millstones might affect the quality of the flour. Horace (*Sat.* i. 89) complained that the bread of Canusium was full of sand. C. T. Ramage (*The Nooks and Byways of South Italy*, 1965 edn., p. 183), visiting Canosa 1,900 years later, made the same complaint, to be told that this was due to the nature of the local millstones.

iv. There were two or three horse-mills in the centre of Cambridge (cf. *Cambridge Borough Documents*, p. 93); one of these *quidam clerici universitatis* had partly demolished in 1286 (in protest against a monopoly?); another was owned by Corpus by 1448. For a water-mill near Merton Hall in Cambridge see J. M. Gray, *The School of Pythagoras* (*CAS* 4º Pubns. N.S. iv (1932)), p. 53.

Fourteenth-century Cambridge guild records name a Henry Scot 'mellere' and Thomas Molendinarius.

APPENDIX C

Merton and Cambridge

MERTON COLLEGE owned land in or near Cambridge for seven centuries, and the names of three houses, a farm, a barn, and a public house still testify to the connection.[1] Walter de Merton, for what purpose we know not, had acquired five distinct properties in the area,[2] including the notable stone house later given the name of Pythagoras Hall. The college treated them as a single manorial unit —a view long threatened by *Quo Warranto* but confirmed whilst Charles I (or rather, Henrietta Maria) was a guest of the college during the Civil War. The college was paying hagable at Cambridge by 1295 (OHS N.S. xviii. 172). From 1321 to 1382 it was farming the property on its own account but in the latter year leased it to a Cambridge burgess, Thomas Trivet. A hagable rental, now in the Bodleian, Gough MS. Camb. 2, p. 427, records that *c.* 1590–1617 Merton paid 4s. 10d.—a very high sum—for Cambridge lands and tenements. A Cambridge mayor, Oliver Flint, held houses in St. Giles Parish 'by copy of court roll of Merton College' in 1586 (*Cambridge Borough Documents*, p. 151). The bailiff of the King's Mill paid up to 20s. hagable to Merton until the eighteenth century, when it became quitrent.[3] The college owned Cop(ped) or Coper Hall, a house in Chesterton lane, till 1835, when it was sold to Magdalene and became the site of the Master's Lodge.

That there were disputes over the extent of Merton manor can be seen from Cooper's *Annals*, and they revived, readers of Maitland's

---

[1] In the grounds of Merton House at Grantchester stands a wall of small round and pointed arches of medieval ecclesiastic character, but not identified by the Commission on Historical Monuments.

[2] Listed and described by J. M. Gray, *The School of Pythagoras* (*CAS* 4° Pubns. N.S. iv, 1932), Section III; see also Highfield, pp. 42–3, and W. Farrer, *Feudal Cambridgeshire* (1920), pp. 177, 211, 249. The land in Cambridge and Chesterton amounted to 97 acres, practically all on the left bank of the river (the college at one time claimed fishing rights as far as mid-stream: see Gray, p. 24); that at Grantchester to (originally) 88 acres. Wheat and drage were the principal crops.

[3] For the origin of this payment see Gray, op. cit., p. 20.

Township and Borough will remember, in the early nineteenth century. As Maitland remarked, the history of this manor could only be written by one of 'the clerks of Merton'. One hopes that the present Librarian may find leisure to write it.

Walter de Merton also acquired for his college lands in Gamlingay, twenty miles to the west of Cambridge, and treated as a separate manor; and the college acquired another four acres there from Richard Dunning, the impecunious former owner of the stone house just mentioned (Gray, p. 9). The Gamlingay estate included a mill (see Highfield, p. 170), and at least once sent pigs over to the Warden's house at Oxford (ibid., p. 62). It was in charge of a bailiff.[1] The accounts of Walter de Cuddington in 1282 (Highfield, p. 285) speak of the 'granges' of Cambridge, Grantchester, and Gamlingay. The sums received from the sale of grain in that year were £12. 12s. 0d., £9. 15s. 6d., and £8. 7s. 6d. respectively.

The Merton Rolls show that wardens, bursars, fellows, and servants regularly rode across to attend to business or supervise harvests on the Cambridge manors: see Highfield, pp. 181, 210, 228, 285 ff., 334, 361. A clause in the statutes governed allowances for expenses on these (two-day) journeys. Those who went to Grantchester would know something about the adjoining manor of Trumpington. The Grantchester mill was part of the Merton property. A bailiff managed this property for the college and the Hundred Rolls give its yearly value as £10. 11s. 2d. The water driving it flowed through Trumpington land, hence we find the college in 1502 paying the lord of Trumpington manor a rent for diverting water into the cut or race leading to Grantchester Mill. King's College, shortly after its foundation, leased land from Merton at Grantchester (including the mill) to ensure its wheat supply: see p. 122 above. At the 1802 enclosures the holdings at Grantchester were redistributed and Merton was allotted land running north from the village along the Cambridge road. Here still stands Merton Barn, recently sold and converted to private use.

---

[1] A membrane in Merton College Roll 5370 (1314) relating to the goods of a deceased bailiff reads: 'Compotus Johanni Schike de bonis Johanni de Seukeworthe nuper defuncti . . . etc. iii d. pro duobus libris de romance venditis.' *Pace* P. S. Allen, *romance* may mean simply 'in French': the books were not necessarily 'romances'. I owe thanks to Dr. Highfield and Mr. J. B. Burgess for a transcript of the entry.

ADDITIONAL NOTES

p. 49. For a guild of St. Nicholas composed of the parish clerks of London city churches, who may have produced plays, see E. K. Chambers, *The Mediaeval Stage* (1903), ii. 118–19.

p. 55. For descriptions of Augustinian granges see Colin Platt, *The Monastic Grange in Medieval England* (1969), Appendix 2.

pp. 63 ff. For Buckingham, Bradwardine, and the Merton School in general see the important collection of studies by Konstanty Michalski, *La Philosophie au XIVᵉ siècle*, ed. Kurt Flasch (Frankfurt, 1969), e.g. pp. 285, 298.

p. 119. Archbishop Courtenay's Statutes for Canterbury College (1384) make provision for 'quinque scolares pauperes, liberi et legitimi, morigerati et ingenio pollentes'. 'It is expected that they will take orders or enter religion, though one or two of them may be allowed to transfer to civil law. Three are to be nominated by the archbishop, two by the prior and chapter of Christ Church Canterbury. They are not *socii*, but recipients of the charity of the college. They are to be given a room, or rooms, and allowed 10d a week for commons. On feast days they are to attend service in chapel, read the lessons and sing *voluntarie quilibet suo modo*. Provided they behave well, they may stay for seven years.' Dr. Pantin prints many of the letters of appointment of these scholars in the fifteenth century: see OHS n.s. viii. 42, 99, 123.

Noblemen's sons would be an exception to the general rule of poverty; but no specific mention of them is found before the Magdalen statutes. The student supported at Oxford by Eynsham Abbey collected and kept the rents of the Eynsham tenements in the town (*Oxoniensia*, xxxvi (1971), 17). He must have lived better than most.

INDEX